NewEdj:
A Business Narrative
Or, the musings of two mad women.

Rachael Evans MA, FCMI

Krysten M. Bacan

*Copyright © 2023 Rachael Evans and Krysten M. Bacan
Cover Design, Layout and Editing: Diane Cullinan
NewEdj Inc. All rights reserved
ISBN 9798864068564*

Foreword

It has truly been my pleasure to witness the evolution of Kyrsten Bacan and Rachael Evans in their entrepreneurial journey. And now to have the honor to pin the foreword for this literary gift. As a Lean Six Sigma Master Black Belt Practitioner, and the owner of my own consulting firm, this topic resonated with me because I use many of the same strategies. When I first connected with them, I knew that they were not your "everyday" techies. Our conversations are rich and not so over the top that I have to get an interpreter. The holistic blend of IT, their world and mine, the rest of the organization have always found that common ground of managing enterprise risk, however it is defined.

It is a NewEdj Way and driven by the IT universe. This book provides an extraordinary journey through the pathway carved by Global Subject Mater Experts Kyrsten Bacan and Rachael Evans. These ladies have taken the entire holistic path of Continuous Improvement and engaged their readers with all of the considerations for attaining sustainable success. And I would be remiss if I did not note the "tools" to use in implementation and oversight.

As a practitioner myself, I always look to explore the role of how IT is integrated into the conversation of business. Krysten and Rachael give you a roadmap using the Waterfall and Agile Project Methodology and merge it with the holistic approach to Enterprise Risk Management. In other words, it is not just about the "wires running through the walls and floors" of your organizations. Being an Organization Transformationist, I truly appreciated the narratives around management focus and style as well as "the people."

This book removes any confusion that often exists in an organization strategy and goal attainment culture. Specifically, the culture and mission are crafted from the top and it is imperative for leadership to be open to its options for a "NewEdj" philosophy for success. This strategy will require a transformationist attitude and also one of being dissatisfied with the status quo. Krysten and Rachael give the reader a reason to cheer because it is laid out for you.

This literary piece is truly one that can become a reference guide for executives and leaders at all levels who have embraced being unsatisfied with mediocrity. It is not a linear view of performance and process excellence, but a global perspective. It reinforced in me that my own conversation is still valid. And if you are a new language to speak, the glossaries shared, and the case studies are user friendly. The later let me know that these ladies have "walked their talk" as shared in this book and not just researched it.

For me, **NewEdj: A Business Narrative** is one for the winner's circle because it truly defines Mission Accomplished for Leaders and Executives regardless of your business, industry of non-profit organization.

Gail P. Birks, EMBA, LMBB President/CEO CMA Enterprise Incorporated

"Rachael and Krysten have provided a concise and practical overview of a number of areas in this book which any current or future manager will find useful and helpful when dealing with similar situations and issues".

Ciaran Ennis, Program Manager, National Broadband Ireland

"NewEdj have compiled a valuable series of whitepapers that is a must read for large or small enterprises who are struggling with managing change in their business. The articles are informative and balanced, providing the reader an honest perspective on the best solution for the individual business. They have also managed to balance the importance of Finance Methodology and People which is no mean-feat."

Cormac Cullinan, Program Director & Six Sigma Black Belt, UNUM Ireland

Introduction

Welcome to this multifaceted anthology of articles and white papers that bridges the intricate dimensions of modern business practices. Authored by Rachael Evans and Krysten Bacan, this collection has been carefully curated to offer an in-depth exploration of two critical domains that shape organisational success—Management and People.

In a time where technological innovation and globalisation continue to redefine the very contours of business, mastering the subtleties of effective management and people-centred practices has become increasingly vital. This book aims to equip its readers with nuanced perspectives and actionable insights, synthesised through rigorous academic research and professional experience.

Management: The Nucleus of Organisational Excellence

The journey commences with an incisive exploration of 'Management', the fulcrum around which all business processes revolve. The focal points within this section span critical issues such as "Cost Management in IT," "Financial Management Competencies for Non-Financial Managers," and "Contractor to Consultant: Can One Become the Other?". These articles delve into the complexities of governance, financial acumen, and role adaptability, providing a robust conceptual framework alongside pragmatic recommendations.

People: The Vital Organisational Resource

Transitioning from the technicalities and hard skills accentuated in the 'Management' section, we pivot to a perhaps even more complex realm—People. Articles in this section explore pressing human-centric challenges such as "Navigating Unresolved Non-Performing Peer Issues" and "Balancing Expertise and Leadership." The intent here is to offer frameworks and solutions that enable a deeper understanding of how human capital can be optimised to create value, both tangibly and intangibly.

Theoretical Depth and Practical Utility

This collection transcends the conventional by seamlessly integrating theory with practice. Each article is substantiated by a strong foundation of academic scholarship, offering not merely descriptive accounts but analytical perspectives that invite critical thought.

Who Should Read This Book?

While this anthology serves as a valuable resource for senior executives and human resource professionals, its breadth and depth make it equally beneficial for middle managers, consultants, and even those aspiring to climb the organisational ladder.

As you engage with the ideas and frameworks presented in this collection, we hope they will catalyse both personal and organisational transformations. Your journey through the complex topography of modern business practices commences herein; may this volume serve as an indispensable guide along the way.

Rachael & Krysten

Biographies

Rachael Evans MA, FCMI

Co-President Biz-Edge and NewEdj

Rachael, the Co-President of our company, specializes in Financial Services, Pharma, operations optimisation and transformation. With a background in banking and technology, she has worked with leading institutions such as HSBC, Credit Suisse, Bank of America, and UBS, as well as at Microsoft and Vodafone. Rachael holds multiple postgraduates and is a Fellow at the Chartered Management Institute, where she continues to contribute her expertise to the field of management. Her guidance and support have helped many businesses achieve their goals and succeed in today's competitive marketplace.

Krysten Bacan

President/Founder Biz-Edge and NewEdj

Meet Krysten, our technology executive and co-founder of NewEdj, with over 20 years of experience in the industry. Throughout her career, she has excelled in technology integration, resource management, and strategic planning. As a CTO/CIO mentor, Krysten has had the privilege of guiding multiple companies through periods of growth and transformation. She has also provided her expertise and leadership in interim roles during times of organizational change. Krysten is a recognized thought leader in her field, and she takes pride in her ability to optimize costs and select and review the best and most appropriate MSPs for her clients.

Table of Contents

Foreward i
Introduction iii
Biographies v

Section 1: Management

1. Comparative Analysis of Waterfall and Agile Project Delivery Methodologies 3
2. Cost Management in IT 21
3. Financial Management Competencies for Non-Financial Managers .. 31
4. Harnessing Smart Processes for Hard Savings 43
5. The Innovation Gap 49
6. The Hidden Cost of Saving 59
7. Redefining Data Security 71
8. Change vs. Project Management 81

Section 2: People

9. Balancing Expertise and Leadership 97
10. Embracing Change 101
11. Contractor to Consultant, can one become the other? 105
12. In-house Knowledge Development and External Consultation 113
13. The Implication of Military Management Techniques for the Commercial Sector 127
14. Navigating Unresolved Non-Performing Peer Issues 139
15. The Reluctant Leader 147

16. The Toxic Employee Dilemma 163
17. Voluntary Participation in Management Coaching 167
18. The Cult of Personality 171

Section One: Management

Rachael Evans MA, FCMI

1. Comparative Analysis of Waterfall and Agile Project Delivery Methodologies: Implementation, Roles, Efficacies, and Selection Criteria

Project management methodologies play a pivotal role in guiding and streamlining processes across various industries. Two prominent methodologies, Waterfall and Agile, offer distinct approaches to project management, Waterfall follows a linear and sequential model, whilst Agile is an iterative and incremental approach.

This paper aims to provide a comprehensive comparison of these methodologies, analyzing their key characteristics, team roles, benefits, and deficiencies. It explores the factors influencing the selection of an appropriate methodology, such as project size, complexity, budget, timeline, and stakeholder engagement. By incorporating various references and practical examples, this paper aims to equip project managers with the knowledge needed to make informed decisions in selecting and implementing project management methodologies. Understanding the differences and strengths of Waterfall and Agile methodologies is crucial in meeting and delivering project objectives effectively.

Introduction:

Project management methodologies play a pivotal role in orchestrating and optimizing processes within a multitude of industries ranging from software development to construction. Amongst a plethora of methodologies, both Waterfall and Agile stand as two of the most prevalent and influential paradigms. Introduced in the 1970s, Waterfall is often regarded as the traditional model for project management. It adopts a linear and sequential approach, where a project is broken down into set phases that must be completed one after another (Royce, 1970). Each phase is contingent upon the deliverables of the previous phase, thus making execution and delivery structured and predetermined.

In comparison, Agile emerged at the beginning of the 21st century as a more dynamic alternative, embodying an iterative and incremental approach to project management. Agile's inception was marked by the publication of the Agile Manifesto in 2001, which focused on flexibility, collaboration, and customer feedback (Beck et al., 2001). Agile methodologies, such as Scrum, break down projects into smaller units, targeted at delivering a more rapid adaptation to change and continuous improvement.

The objective of this paper is to provide an attempt to critically examine and compare these two distinct methodologies, shedding light on their underlying principles, structures, and application areas. Moreover, I delve into the key roles within each methodology, along with the associated benefits and deficiencies. A focal point of my analysis is to elucidate the contexts and scenarios in which each methodology excels and provide insights on how to select the appropriate methodology based on project attributes such as size, complexity, stakeholder requirements, and risk factors. Through the synthesis of the literature, case studies, and practical examples, my paper aims to equip project managers and stakeholders with the knowledge and tools needed to make informed decisions in the selection and implementation of project management methodologies.

Waterfall Methodology

The Waterfall methodology is traditionally associated with software development but has been employed across various sectors. As previously mentioned, it is a linear and sequential approach, and the term "Waterfall" signifies the way the process cascades down through various stages. The model was first formalized by Dr Winston W. Royce in 1970 (Royce, 1970).

Key Phases of Waterfall Projects:

1. <u>Requirements</u>: In this phase, all the requirements for the project are gathered and documented. It is vital that the requirements are as detailed and clear as possible as the rest of the project is built on this foundation. This phase includes understanding the client's needs and ensuring that the stakeholders have a shared understanding of the objectives and constraints.

2. <u>Design</u>: Once the requirements are clearly understood, the project moves into the design phase. This phase involves creating detailed specifications and design documents, which guide the rest of the development. For software projects, this phase includes system architecture and user interface design.

3. <u>Implementation</u>: Based on the design specifications, the actual code is developed, or the main product is built during this phase. It is also commonly referred to as the development phase. Here, the focus is on building the product according to the specifications laid out in the design phase.

4. <u>Integration and Testing</u>: Once the product is built, it is assembled and tested as a coherent unit. In software development, this phase involves not only testing individual parts (unit testing) but also the interactions between the parts (integration testing) and the system (system testing).
5. <u>Deployment</u>: After thorough testing, the product is deployed to the production environment. For software products, this means releasing the software to the users. In the case of physical products, this phase includes manufacturing and distribution.
6. <u>Maintenance</u>: Post-deployment, the product enters the maintenance phase where it will receive updates and fixes. This phase ensures that the product continues to perform and meet its objectives in a live environment.

Characteristics of the Waterfall Model:

- <u>Sequential Nature</u>: As mentioned earlier, each phase must be fully completed before the next begins, which makes the process rigid.
- <u>Emphasis on Documentation</u>: Each phase results in detailed documentation before moving on to the next stage.
- <u>Dependency</u>: The success of each phase is dependent on the one preceding it, as each phase is built upon the deliverables of the previous phase.
- <u>Difficult to Accommodate Changes</u>: Once the project progresses beyond a phase, it is usually very difficult and expensive to go back and make changes.

Team Roles in Waterfall

In the Waterfall model, each phase has specific tasks and objectives. This necessitates different roles within the team to efficiently handle these tasks. Below is an expanded overview of the team roles involved in a typical Waterfall model project:

Project Manager:

<u>Responsibilities</u>: The Project Manager is responsible for the overall planning, execution, and completion of the project. This includes defining the project scope, developing a project schedule, allocating resources, and managing

risks. Additionally, they are responsible for ensuring that the project is delivered on time, within scope, and within budget.

Skills: A Project Manager should possess strong leadership skills, the ability to communicate effectively, excellent organizational skills, and a good understanding of the project domain.

System Analyst:

Responsibilities: The System Analyst plays a crucial role in the requirements and design phase of the Waterfall model. They are responsible for understanding the business requirements, analyzing the needs of the end-users, and translating them into technical specifications. This includes creating detailed requirement documents and ensuring that the developed system aligns with the business objectives.

Skills: Analytical thinking, problem-solving, effective communication, and a deep understanding of both business and technical aspects are essential skills for a System Analyst.

Designers:

Responsibilities: Designers are primarily involved in the design phase. In software development, for instance, this includes creating the system architecture, database schema, and user interface design. They should ensure that the design meets the requirements and is feasible within the constraints of the project.

Skills: Creative thinking, proficiency in design tools, understanding of user experience (UX) principles, and knowledge of the project domain are essential for Designers.

Developers:

Responsibilities: Developers, also known as Programmers or Coders, are responsible for the implementation phase. They write the code or build the main product according to the specifications laid out in the design phase. They must adhere to coding standards and ensure that the product is built according to the requirements.

Skills: Developers need to have strong programming skills, problem-solving abilities, and knowledge of algorithms and data structures. They also need to be proficient in the programming languages and tools relevant to the project.

Testers:

Responsibilities: Testers are involved in the integration and testing phase of the Waterfall model. They are responsible for testing the product to ensure it meets the requirements and is free of defects. This includes creating test plans, executing tests, and documenting the results.

Skills: *Attention to detail, analytical thinking, proficiency in testing tools and methodologies, and the ability to communicate findings effectively are important skills for Testers.*

Benefits:

1. Clear Structure and Phases (Sommerville, 2011): The Waterfall models linear approach ensures that there is a clear demarcation between the different phases of the project. Each phase has specific deliverables and a review process which helps in creating an organized structure. This clarity allows stakeholders to have a better understanding of the milestones and the overall roadmap of the project.

2. Suitable for Small Projects with Well-defined Requirements: In cases where the project is small and the requirements are well-understood and fixed, the Waterfall model can be an efficient choice. Its straightforward nature allows for quicker development since the focus stays on execution without the need for constant evaluation and changes.

3. Easy to Manage: Given its structured nature, the Waterfall model is relatively easy to manage. Since each phase has specific deliverables and a review process, it can be simpler to measure progress and ensure adherence to quality standards. The emphasis on documentation further ensures that there is ample reference material available for every phase, making it easier for team members to understand what is expected at each stage.

Deficiencies:

1. Rigid Structure; Difficult to Accommodate Changes (Boehm, 1988): One of the major drawbacks of the Waterfall model is its lack of flexibility. Once a phase is completed, it is usually very difficult or impossible to go back and make changes without disrupting the whole process. This makes it problematic for projects where requirements may evolve or change during development.

2. Not Suitable for Large and Complex Projects: For large projects with inherent complexity, the Waterfall model may not be ideal. The difficulty in accurately defining the requirements and scope at the beginning of such projects and the inability of the Waterfall model to adapt to changes or unknown factors as they arise makes it less suitable for large-scale endeavors.

3. Extended Time to Market: Since the Waterfall model does not produce a working version of the project until late in the life cycle, it often leads to a longer time to market compared to more iterative approaches. This can be a disadvantage in a competitive market where quick product releases are crucial.

4. Risk of Late Failure: As testing is conducted in the later stages of the project, there are chances of discovering major issues late in the development process. This can sometimes lead to project failure, or extensive, costly last-minute modifications.

The Waterfall model is most effective when the scope of the project is clearly defined and unlikely to change, the technology and tools are well understood, and the project is relatively short in duration. However, its rigidity and late-stage testing make it less ideal for larger, more complex projects, or those in rapidly evolving environments.

Agile Methodology

Agile methodology is an alternative to traditional project management approaches, such as the Waterfall model. It is primarily used in software development but has been adapted to various fields. Agile promotes an iterative and incremental approach, which emphasizes flexibility, collaboration, customer feedback, and rapid releases. The Agile Manifesto, published in 2001, laid the foundation for Agile, outlining its core values and principles (Beck et al., 2001).

Key Phases:

1. Requirements: Agile approaches acknowledge that customer needs may change over time. Therefore, the requirements are often high-level and evolve as the project progresses. Teams are expected to collaborate closely with stakeholders to understand and prioritize their needs.

2. Planning: In Agile, planning is an ongoing activity. The work is divided into small, manageable units known as iterations. Each iteration is planned separately, allowing the team to adapt as necessary. This approach contrasts with Waterfall, where comprehensive planning is conducted at the beginning.
3. Design: Design in Agile is often concurrent with other phases. It emphasizes simplicity and readiness to adapt to changes. It may include creating mock-ups, prototypes, or other visual aids to facilitate understanding and feedback.
4. Development: Development in Agile focuses on producing working features in small increments. The goal is to have a potentially shippable product at the end of each iteration. Continuous integration, code reviews, and other practices are often used to maintain high quality.
5. Testing: Testing in Agile is integrated throughout the lifecycle, instead of being a single phase. This approach, known as continuous testing, allows for early detection of issues and ensures that the product meets the requirements at all stages of development.
6. Deployment: Agile approaches typically include continuous deployment or frequent releases of the product to a production environment. This allows stakeholders to see progress in real-time and provide feedback that can be incorporated in subsequent iterations.
7. Review: At the end of each iteration, the team holds a review meeting to demonstrate the work completed during the iteration to stakeholders. This is also an opportunity for feedback and discussion about what the team should focus on next.

Characteristics of the Agile Methodology:

1. Iterative and Incremental: Agile embraces an iterative and incremental approach to project management. Instead of completing the entire project in sequential phases, it focuses on delivering small increments of functionality in short iterations called sprints.
2. Adaptive and Flexible: Agile methodologies are designed to adapt and respond to changes in requirements, priorities, and project environments. It allows for continuous refinement and reprioritisation of project tasks, making it more flexible compared to the Waterfall model.

3. Emphasis on Collaboration: Agile promotes collaboration among cross-functional teams and encourages the active involvement of stakeholders throughout the project. Collaboration enhances transparency, communication, and collective decision-making, fostering a sense of ownership and shared responsibility.
4. Customer-Centric: Agile methodologies prioritise customer satisfaction and engagement. It involves regular customer feedback and incorporates it into the development process, ensuring that the final product meets customer needs and expectations.
5. Continuous Improvement: Agile encourages continuous improvement through regular reflection and adaptation. Retrospectives at the end of each iteration allow the team to identify areas of improvement and make necessary adjustments for future iterations.
6. Self-Organising Teams: Agile empowers self-organising teams, where individuals collaborate and make collective decisions. Team members have autonomy and accountability, fostering a sense of ownership and motivation.

These characteristics of the Agile methodology stand in contrast to the rigid and sequential nature of the Waterfall model. Agile's adaptability, flexibility, customer-centric focus, and emphasis on collaboration make it particularly suitable for projects with evolving requirements, where feedback-driven iterations and continuous improvement are paramount.

Team Roles in Agile

Product Owner:

Responsibilities: The Product Owner is a key stakeholder in Agile projects and serves as the voice of the customer. They are responsible for defining and prioritising the product backlog, which is a list of features, bug fixes, enhancements, and other tasks that the team will work on. The Product Owner ensures that the backlog items are clearly defined and aligned with the business goals. They also collaborate with the development team to provide clarification on requirements and accept or reject the work results.

Skills: A Product Owner should possess strong communication skills, have a clear understanding of the customer's needs, be knowledgeable in product management, and can make decisions that align with both the customer's interests and the business goals.

Scrum Master:

Responsibilities: The Scrum Master is often considered a servant-leader for the Agile team, as they help to facilitate the Scrum process. They ensure that the team is following Agile practices, and they help remove any obstacles that the team may be facing. The Scrum Master also works to ensure that the development environment is conducive for the team to work efficiently, and they facilitate meetings like daily stand-ups and sprint reviews.

Skills: A Scrum Master needs to have a good understanding of Agile principles and practices, be skilled in conflict resolution, possess strong facilitation and communication skills, and can work with both the development team and stakeholders to ensure a smooth development process.

Development Team Members:

Responsibilities: Development Team Members are responsible for delivering potentially shippable product increments at the end of each sprint or iteration. In Agile, the development team is cross-functional, meaning it includes professionals with various expertise needed to complete the project. This includes not just coders, but often QA testers, designers, and sometimes business analysts. Development Team Members are responsible for estimating tasks, developing features, testing, and ensuring that the product meets the acceptance criteria.

Skills: Development Team Members should be skilled in their respective domains, whether that be coding, design, testing and so on. They should also be collaborative, be able to work in a fast-paced environment and be open to changing requirements.

In Agile methodologies, team collaboration and communication are highly valued. The roles are more integrated, with team members often wearing multiple hats, and there is a greater focus on delivering a product that meets customer needs and can adapt as those needs change.

Benefits:

1. Flexibility and Adaptability: Agile methodologies are designed to adapt to changes in requirements or the project environment. Through iterative cycles, Agile teams can quickly incorporate feedback and make necessary adjustments. This adaptability is particularly beneficial in fast-paced or uncertain environments where requirements may evolve over time. (Highsmith & Cockburn, 2001)

2. <u>Rapid Release of Usable Product Features</u>: Agile emphasises delivering small, incremental releases of the product with each iteration. This allows stakeholders to see progress and start using features earlier than they could in traditional Waterfall projects. Early access to features also enables quicker validation and reduces the time to market.

3. <u>Collaboration and Customer Satisfaction</u>: Agile promotes close collaboration among cross-functional teams and stakeholders. Regular communication and feedback loops ensure that the customer's voice is heard throughout the development process. As a result, the final product is more likely to meet customer needs and expectations, leading to higher levels of satisfaction.

Deficiencies:

1. <u>Can Be Less Predictable</u>: Due to its adaptive nature, Agile can sometimes be less predictable in terms of timelines and budgets. The focus on flexibility and responding to changes can lead to fluctuations in the project's scope, making it harder to provide precise estimates for completion.

2. <u>Less Emphasis on Documentation</u>: Agile methodologies often prioritise working products over comprehensive documentation. While this can speed up development, it might sometimes result in insufficient documentation, making it more difficult for new team members to understand the project or for the team to maintain and upgrade the product in the long term.

3. <u>Not Suitable for Projects with Rigid Structures</u>: For projects that have well-defined requirements and little to no change expected, or where regulatory compliance requires a more structured and documented approach, Agile may not be the best fit. The informal nature of Agile might not satisfy the demands of projects where extensive documentation and strict adherence to specifications are necessary.

Key Differences Between Waterfall and Agile

Having outlined the fundamental principles of both Waterfall and Agile methodologies, it becomes imperative to discern the distinctions between these two approaches as they differ substantially in their execution and management styles. Understanding these differences is paramount for project managers and stakeholders, as the choice between Waterfall and Agile can have a significant impact on how effectively a project meets its objectives (Stoica, Mircea & Ghilic-Micu, 2013). This section delves into the core differences between Waterfall and Agile methodologies in terms of structure, adaptability, team roles, and customer engagement. By contrasting these methodologies in these domains, this section aims to furnish readers with the insights needed to make informed decisions regarding the appropriate methodology tailored to the specific needs and constraints of their projects.

Structure:

Waterfall: Waterfall is characterised by a linear and sequential structure where progress flows in one direction—downward through various phases such as conception, initiation, analysis, design, construction, testing, deployment, and maintenance. Each phase must be completed before the next phase begins, and there is little room for revisiting a phase once it has been completed (Larson & Chang, 2016).

Agile: Agile, on the other hand, adopts an iterative structure. It divides the project into small increments. The project team works on the complete development cycle (from conception to deployment) for a small part of the software in short iterations, called sprints, usually lasting two to four weeks. This means that the software is built incrementally from the start of the project, instead of trying to deliver it all at once near the end.

Adaptability:

Waterfall: Because of its rigid structure, adapting to changes in project requirements can be very difficult and costly once the project is underway in the Waterfall methodology.

Agile: Agile is designed to be highly adaptable, allowing for changes to be made after the initial planning. Throughout the project, teams can reassess project priorities and direction at regular intervals, allowing them to adapt to changes and evolve the project as needed.

Team Roles:

Waterfall: In Waterfall methodology, team roles are highly specialised, and each phase typically has distinct roles. For example, system analysts are active mainly during the requirements and design stages, while testers are active during the testing phase. Communication between phases is often limited.

Agile: Agile promotes cross-functional teams, meaning that individuals in the team may play multiple roles. Additionally, Agile encourages continuous

1. Comparative Analysis of Waterfall and Agile

communication among all team members and involves the customer throughout the development. Scrum Master and Product Owner are examples of specialised roles in Agile.

Customer Engagement:

Waterfall: Customer engagement in Waterfall is generally limited to the beginning and end of the project. The customer's requirements are gathered at the beginning of the project, and the final product is delivered at the end, with little customer involvement in between.

Agile: Agile involves continuous customer feedback throughout the development process. Regular interactions with the customer or stakeholder are encouraged for better understanding and incorporation of the customer's requirements and feedback into the product.

Whilst Waterfall's structured approach can be beneficial for projects with well-defined requirements, its rigid structure is often seen as a disadvantage for projects in fast-paced environments. Agile, with its emphasis on flexibility, collaboration, and customer engagement, is often more suited to projects where there is a high degree of change and uncertainty.

Variations in Model Execution & Delivery

In project management, the process of efficiently navigating through various phases of a project involves critical aspects such as planning, monitoring, communications, and post-project reviews. These elements are instrumental in determining the success and effectiveness of any project. In this section, we will delve into each of these components and explore how they are approached within the Waterfall and Agile methodologies.

Planning is the bedrock upon which projects are built, entailing the establishment of objectives, scope, resources, and timelines. Monitoring involves the ongoing evaluation of project performance and making necessary adjustments to ensure alignment with goals. Communications encompass the mechanisms and channels for information dissemination amongst stakeholders, vital for coordinated effort and decision-making. Lastly, post-project reviews constitute a reflective analysis upon the completion of the project to assess outcomes, and efficiencies, and glean insights for future endeavours.

Understanding the distinctions in how these critical elements are handled in

Waterfall and Agile methodologies provides invaluable insights for project managers and stakeholders in tailoring their approach to the unique demands and attributes of their projects.

Planning:

Waterfall: In the Waterfall methodology, planning is a critical phase that occurs at the beginning of the project. Extensive and meticulous upfront planning is required, including defining the scope, setting objectives, allocating resources, and creating timelines. This approach seeks to outline the entirety of the project in detail before the work commences, which leaves little room for deviation or changes later on (Cobb, 2011).

Agile: Contrasting with Waterfall, Agile acknowledges that planning is an ongoing activity. Initial planning is less extensive, and the project is allowed to evolve as it progresses. Agile teams frequently reassess and modify plans to ensure that the project adapts to any changes or newly surfaced information.

Monitoring:

Waterfall: Monitoring in Waterfall methodology is generally milestone-based. Progress is measured against the initial plan, and monitoring is less frequent, often occurring at the end of each phase. There is limited opportunity to make significant changes once a phase is complete.

Agile: Agile incorporates more frequent and informal monitoring. The common practice is to have daily stand-up meetings where the team discusses progress, plans for the day, and any impediments. This allows for real-time assessment and rapid response to issues or changes.

Communications:

Waterfall: Waterfall typically follows a more hierarchical and formal communication structure. Information tends to flow from the top down, and communication across different departments or phases is often limited. This formality can sometimes hinder swift decision-making.

Agile: In Agile, communication is viewed as a vital element. Agile emphasises open, transparent, and continuous communication among all team members. The constant exchange of information allows for collaborative decision-making and ensures that the team stays aligned with the customer's needs and project goals.

Post-Project Reviews:

Waterfall: In Waterfall, a post-project review is conducted after the project is completed. This review evaluates the project against the original objectives, budget, and schedule. It is a reflective process, aimed at identifying lessons learned for future projects.

Agile: Agile methodologies incorporate regular reviews at the end of each iteration or sprint. These reviews are not just reflective but also feed into the planning for the next iteration. This allows the project to adapt and evolve based on feedback and assessment throughout its lifecycle, rather than just at the end.

Selection Process and Considerations

The choice between Agile and Waterfall methodologies often depends on several key factors, each having distinct implications for project execution and outcome. Deciding the appropriate approach requires careful consideration of the project's context, resources, and goals (Wysocki, 2014).

Project Size and Complexity: Large, complex projects may benefit from Agile's iterative and incremental approach, as it allows for regular inspection of the project's progress and provides opportunities to adjust direction based on the lessons learned. On the contrary, smaller projects with less complexity might be effectively managed using the Waterfall methodology, given its straightforward and linear nature.

Budget and Timeline: Projects with a tight budget and strict timelines may find the Waterfall approach more appropriate. Its sequential nature allows for a detailed plan outlining the cost and schedule upfront, offering more predictability. Agile, on the other hand, accommodates change and uncertainty but could potentially extend the project timeline and budget due to its iterative approach.

Stakeholder Engagement: Agile's emphasis on customer collaboration suits project where constant stakeholder engagement is desired or necessary. Regular feedback in Agile can lead to a product more aligned with user needs. In contrast, Waterfall is structured with minimal customer involvement during the development process, mostly at the start and end of the project.

Requirements Stability: Agile is adept at handling projects with evolving or ambiguous requirements due to its inherent flexibility. It allows continuous refinement and reprioritisation of the product backlog. In contrast, Waterfall is more suited for projects with stable, well-defined, and understood requirements right from the start.

Risk Management: Agile's frequent iterations allow risks to be identified and addressed quickly, making it suitable for projects with a high degree of uncertainty and risk. Waterfall, with its focus on comprehensive documentation and upfront planning, might be a more fitting choice for projects where risk needs to be meticulously assessed and mitigated beforehand.

Thus, whilst Agile is typically preferred for projects that require flexibility, and customer engagement, and are of a larger scale with potential for changes in scope, Waterfall can be more suited to projects with well-defined, unchanging requirements, smaller scale, tight budget control, and minimal stakeholder engagement. It is essential for project managers to evaluate the project characteristics and stakeholder preferences carefully to select the most appropriate methodology.

Conclusion

The nature of project environments necessitates the employment of robust and effective project management methodologies. This paper engaged in an in-depth examination of two of the most widely used methodologies, Waterfall and Agile. Through a comprehensive analysis, it has been highlighted that both methodologies offer unique advantages and are accompanied by certain limitations.

Waterfall, with its linear and structured approach, offers clarity and simplicity, making it suitable for projects with well-defined requirements and minimal changes expected. Agile, on the other hand, is characterised by its flexibility, adaptability, and emphasis on collaboration and customer feedback, making it an ideal choice for projects with uncertain or evolving requirements.

The selection between Waterfall and Agile should not be seen as a binary choice, but rather a strategic decision based on a multitude of factors such as project size, complexity, stakeholder engagement, budget, and timeline. Moreover, it is important to recognise that the landscape of project management is not static. Hybrid approaches, which blend elements of both Waterfall and Agile, are emerging and can offer pragmatic solutions tailored to specific project needs.

As project environments continue to evolve, it becomes imperative for project managers and stakeholders to not only understand these methodologies but also to remain adaptable and open to emerging practices and methodologies.

For future research, it would be valuable to explore how hybrid methodologies are being employed in various industries, and how they can be optimised to address the unique challenges faced by different types of projects. Additionally, examining the role of emerging technologies in project management and how they can be integrated within Waterfall, Agile, or hybrid methodologies could provide insightful contributions to the field.

Waterfall and Agile methodologies are both in themselves powerful tools in the arsenal of project management. Understanding their strengths, limitations, and applications can empower project managers to make informed decisions that align with the project's objectives, stakeholder expectations, and operational constraints.

References

Beck, K., Beedle, M., van Bennekum, A., Cockburn, A., Cunningham, W., Fowler, M., ... & Kern, J. (2001). Manifesto for agile software development.

Boehm, B. W. (1988). A spiral model of software development and enhancement. ACM SIGSOFT Software Engineering Notes, 11(4), 14-24.

Cobb, C. G. (2011). Making sense of agile project management: balancing control and agility. John Wiley & Sons.

Highsmith, J., & Cockburn, A. (2001). Agile software development: The business of innovation. Computer, 34(9), 120-122.

Larson, D., & Chang, V. (2016). A review and future direction of agile, business intelligence, analytics and data science. International Journal of Information Management, 36(5), 700-710.

Pressman, R. S. (2014). Software Engineering: A Practitioner's Approach. McGraw-Hill Education.

Royce, W. W. (1970). Managing the development of large software systems. Proceedings of IEEE WESCON, 1-9.

Sommerville, I. (2011). Software Engineering. Addison-Wesley.

Stoica, M., Mircea, M., & Ghilic-Micu, B. (2013). Software Development: Agile vs. Traditional. Informatica Economica, 17(4), 64-76.

Wysocki, R. K. (2014). Effective project management: traditional, agile, extreme. John Wiley & Sons.

Rachael Evans MA, FCMI & Krysten M. Bacan

2. Cost Management in IT: Strategies for Identifying Opportunities and Optimising Expenses

Effective cost management is essential for organisations to navigate budgetary constraints and foster growth. This brief paper explores the significance of cost management in organisations, with a specific focus on IT costs. It provides strategies for identifying cost saving opportunities and managing IT expenses efficiently. The research outcomes emphasise the importance of considering technology, process, and people aspects in achieving optimal cost management. By leveraging examples and research references, it offers practical insights and recommendations for organisations seeking to overcome budgetary limitations while ensuring sustainable growth. From conducting cost analyses and leveraging technology for cost reduction to optimising IT asset management, the paper explores various strategies and best practices.

This paper further highlights the significance of prioritising cost reduction initiatives, implementing effective procurement practices, and monitoring IT expenditure. Furthermore, the paper discusses technology considerations, such as cost-effective infrastructure solutions, IT service management tools, and cloud computing for cost optimisation. Process considerations, including lean and agile practices, IT governance, and project management, are also addressed. Lastly, the paper emphasises the importance of creating a cost-conscious culture and effective IT leadership. Through the presentation of case studies and examples, this paper provides a comprehensive frame-work to help organisations identify cost-saving opportunities, manage IT costs effectively, and foster sustainable growth in the face of budgetary constraints.

Introduction

Cost management plays a critical role in organisations by enabling them to achieve financial stability, maximise profitability, and foster sustainable growth (Atkinson, Kaplan, & Young, 2019). In an increasingly competitive business landscape, organisations must proactively identify cost-saving opportunities and implement effective strategies to manage their expenses (Kouki, 2018). The observations and findings focus on cost management in the context of Information Technology (IT) and explore how organisations can navigate budgetary constraints while ensuring optimal utilisation of IT resources.

The primary outcome of this paper is therefore to provide practical guidance on identifying cost-saving opportunities and managing IT costs effectively. It emphasises the importance of technology, process, and people considerations in achieving cost management goals. The paper will delve into various strategies and best practices that organisations can adopt to streamline their IT expenses and achieve financial efficiency.

Identifying Cost-Saving Opportunities

Effective cost management is crucial for organisations to achieve financial stability, maximise profitability, and foster sustainable growth. In the realm of Information Technology (IT), organisations face the challenge of managing costs while leveraging technology to drive innovation and competitive advantage. This section delves into key strategies for identifying cost-saving opportunities and managing IT costs effectively, considering technology, process, and people considerations.

Conducting a Cost Analysis

Before implementing cost-saving initiatives, organisations must conduct a comprehensive cost analysis. This analysis involves identifying different cost categories and understanding the key cost drivers within each category. By conducting a detailed examination of expenditures, organisations can pinpoint inefficiencies, redundancies, and areas where costs can be reduced (Langabeer II, 2018).

Leveraging Technology for Cost Reduction

Technology plays a pivotal role in cost reduction efforts. Organisations can explore automation and process streamlining to eliminate manual and time-consuming tasks, thereby reducing labour costs (Chang, Chien, & Yang, 2019). Virtualisation and cloud computing can provide opportunities for infrastructure consolidation and resource optimisation, leading to significant cost savings (Sharma & Mishra, 2021).

Optimising IT Asset Management

IT assets, including hardware and software, can be a significant cost driver. Organisations should conduct regular audits to identify underutilised or redundant assets. Rationalising hardware and software can reduce maintenance costs, software licensing fees, and support expenses (Fitzgerald & Stol, 2019). Implementing effective software license management processes can help organisations avoid penalties and optimise licensing costs (Eisenhauer, 2020).

Strategies for Managing IT Costs Effectively

To effectively manage IT costs, organisations must implement strategies that prioritise cost reduction initiatives, adopt effective procurement practices, and establish robust monitoring and control mechanisms. The findings focus on key considerations for managing IT costs and to illustrate the importance of prioritisation, strategic procurement, and effective expenditure monitoring.

Prioritising Cost Reduction Initiatives

To effectively manage IT costs, organisations should prioritise cost reduction initiatives based on their potential impact. Total Cost of Ownership (TCO) analysis helps in evaluating the overall costs associated with IT investments, enabling organisations to make informed decisions (Weill & Broadbent, 2019).

Cost-benefit analysis can further assist in assessing the value proposition of IT projects and investments (Kumar & Das, 2017).

Implementing Effective Procurement Practices

Adopting strategic procurement practices can yield significant cost savings. Careful vendor selection and negotiation can lead to favourable terms, discounts, and pricing structures (Borgman & Dornheim, 2021). Contract management and optimisation can ensure that organisations are not overspending on unnecessary services and that contracts align with their actual requirements (Schöttle & Duller, 2020).

Monitoring and Controlling IT Expenditure

Monitoring and controlling IT expenditure is essential to maintain cost discipline. Organisations should establish robust budgeting and forecasting techniques to track and control expenses effectively. Regular performance tracking and reporting help identify cost variances and deviations, enabling timely corrective actions to be taken (Kotabe, 2018).

Technology Considerations for Cost Management

In the pursuit of effective cost management, organisations can explore various strategies and technologies to achieve cost optimisation within their IT infrastructure. The focus of this section is the identification and delivery of cost-effective infrastructure solutions, the implementation of IT Service Management (ITSM) tools, and the cost optimisation potential offered by cloud computing.

Cost-Effective Infrastructure Solutions

Organisations can explore cost-effective infrastructure solutions, such as virtualisation and consolidation. These technologies enable efficient utilisation of resources, reducing hardware costs, power consumption, and data centre space requirements (Casado & Hussain, 2020). Additionally, software-defined networking (SDN) can provide cost-effective network management and optimisation (Gharaibeh et al., 2019).

IT Service Management (ITSM) Tools

Implementing IT Service Management (ITSM) tools can enhance cost management efforts. Incident management and problem-resolution processes can minimise downtime, reducing associated costs (Ferguson & Roper, 2018). Change and release management practices can ensure smooth transitions and minimise disruptions, mitigating potential costs related to system failures or performance issues (Krämer, 2019).

Cost Optimisation through Cloud Computing

Cloud computing offers opportunities for cost optimisation. Organisations can consider cloud migration strategies to shift from traditional infrastructure to cloud-based services. Right-sizing instances and optimising workloads in the cloud can result in significant cost savings by eliminating the need to invest in and maintain on-premises infrastructure (Marston et al., 2011).

Process Considerations for Cost Management

In the pursuit of effective cost management, organisations can adopt various practices and frameworks that optimise processes, ensure compliance, and enhance project management and delivery. In this section the focus is on the implementation of lean and agile practices, effective IT governance and compliance and the importance of project management and delivery in achieving cost management goals.

Lean and Agile Practices

Implementing lean and agile practices can drive cost management initiatives. By optimising processes and reducing waste, organisations can improve operational efficiency and lower costs (Sánchez, Medina-López, & Romero, 2019). Continuous improvement methodologies, such as Kaizen or Six Sigma, can facilitate ongoing cost-reduction efforts (Zhang, Sarker, & Basu, 2017).

IT Governance and Compliance

Effective IT governance and compliance practices are vital for cost management. Ensuring regulatory and security compliance minimises the risks of non-compliance penalties and security breaches, which can be costly (Janssen, 2020). Robust risk management and mitigation practices can help identify potential cost drivers and implement preventive measures (Van Grembergen et al., 2019).

Project Management and Delivery

Effective project management and delivery practices contribute to cost management. Accurate project planning, resource allocation, and scope management prevent cost overruns (Schwalbe, 2020). Organisations should emphasise cost control measures throughout the project lifecycle, ensuring that projects are delivered within budgetary constraints (Pinto, 2020).

People Considerations for Cost Management

Creating a cost-conscious culture and effective IT leadership are fundamental aspects of successful cost management within organisations. Here we highlight the importance of fostering a cost-conscious culture where employees actively participate in cost-saving efforts and emphasise the role of strong IT leadership in aligning IT objectives with broader business goals.

Creating a Cost-Conscious Culture

Organisations should foster a cost-conscious culture where employees actively participate in cost-saving efforts. Conducting employee training programs and raising awareness about cost management initiatives can help generate ideas and encourage cost-saving behaviours (Ireland & Webb, 2017). Recognising and incentivising employees for their contributions to cost-reduction efforts can further enhance engagement (Ferreira, Lages, & Morgado, 2018).

Effective IT Leadership

Strong IT leadership is crucial for successful cost management. IT leaders should align IT objectives with broader business goals, ensuring that cost management strategies are integrated into organisational strategies (Henderson, Venkatraman, & Oldach, 2018). Building cross-functional collaboration between IT and other departments facilitates cost optimisation initiatives and supports organisational objectives (Mahadevan, 2019).

Conclusion

Effective cost management plays a crucial role in enabling organisations to overcome budgetary constraints and drive sustainable growth. By actively identifying cost-saving opportunities and implementing tailored strategies for IT cost management, organisations can optimise their expenses while aligning with their broader business objectives. However, successful cost management goes beyond simple cost-cutting measures. It requires organisations to consider technology, process, and people considerations in their efforts.

Technology considerations involve leveraging technological advancements and solutions to drive cost reduction. This includes exploring automation, virtualisation, and cloud computing to streamline operations, optimise resource utilisation, and reduce hardware and maintenance costs (Chang, Chien, & Yang, 2019; Sharma & Mishra, 2021). By embracing cost-effective infrastructure solutions and implementing IT service management tools, organisations can enhance their cost-management efforts and achieve greater efficiency (Casado & Hussain, 2020; Ferguson & Roper, 2018).

Process considerations are equally important in effective cost management. Implementing lean and agile practices allows organisations to optimise processes, reduce waste, and improve operational efficiency, ultimately leading to lower costs (Sánchez, Medina-López, & Romero, 2019). Additionally, effective IT governance and compliance practices ensure that organisations adhere to regulations, minimise risks, and avoid costly penalties (Janssen, 2020). Project management and delivery practices, including accurate planning, resource allocation, and scope management, prevent cost overruns and ensure projects are delivered within budget (Schwalbe, 2020).

However, people's considerations should not be overlooked. Fostering a cost-conscious culture where employees actively participate in cost-saving efforts can generate valuable ideas and encourage cost-saving behaviours (Ireland & Webb, 2017). Recognising and incentivising employees for their contributions to cost-reduction efforts further enhances engagement and motivation (Ferreira, Lages, & Morgado, 2018). Strong IT leadership is crucial in aligning IT objectives with business goals, integrating cost management strategies into organisational strategies, and fostering collaboration between IT and other departments (Henderson, Venkatraman, & Oldach, 2018; Mahadevan, 2019).

As organisations continue to navigate the evolving business landscape, cost management will remain a fundamental aspect of achieving financial efficiency and long-term success. By adopting a comprehensive approach that considers technology, process, and people considerations, organisations can achieve comprehensive and sustainable cost reduction. Through proactive identification of cost-saving opportunities, implementation of effective strategies, and fostering a cost-conscious culture, organisations can optimise their expenses while supporting their overall business objectives. By embracing cost management as an ongoing practice, organisations can adapt to changing environments and ensure financial stability in the face of evolving budgetary constraints.

References

Atkinson, A. A., Kaplan, R. S., & Young, S. M. (2019). *Management accounting: Information for decision-making and strategy execution.* Pearson.

Borgman, H. P., & Dornheim, S. (2021). The strategic role of procurement in achieving cost reduction. *Journal of Purchasing and Supply Management, 27*(1), 100648.

Casado, L. G., & Hussain, Z. (2020). A survey on virtualisation -based techniques for energyefficient data centers. *Sustainable Computing: Informatics and Systems, 28,* 100446.

Chang, Y., Chien, S., & Yang, C. (2019). Business process automation and financial performance: An empirical investigation. *Information & Management, 56*(1), 103145.

Eisenhauer, M. (2020). Software license management in practice. *Journal of Information Technology Management, 31(1),* 5-17.

Ferguson, C., & Roper, A. (2018). IT service management: Practices, challenges, and implications for practice. *Journal of Information Technology Case and Application Research, 20(2),* 70-86.

Ferreira, A., Lages, C., & Morgado, A. (2018). Incentivising employee engagement in cost reduction: The role of reward systems. *Journal of Business Research, 85,* 449-460.

Fitzgerald, J., & Stol, K. (2019). IT asset management: It's all about process. *Cutter Business Technology Journal, 32(5),* 23-28.

Gharaibeh, S., Al-Qudah, M., Al-Zubi, R., & Jararweh, Y. (2019). Software-defined networking: A comprehensive survey. *Journal of Network and Computer Applications, 127,* 54-84.

Henderson, J. C., Venkatraman, N., & Oldach, S. H. (2018). Speed, strategic choice, and the management of IT in the 21st century. *MIS Quarterly, 42(2),* 627-648.

Ireland, R. D., & Webb, J. W. (2017). A multilevel model of employee innovation: Understanding the effects of regulatory focus, thriving, and employee involvement climate. *Journal of Management, 43(4),* 1085-1109.

Janssen, M. (2020). *Digital government: Concepts and practices.* Springer.

Kotabe, M. (2018). *Corporate strategy: A focused approach.* Cambridge University Press.

Kouki, R. (2018). Cost management: A strategic emphasis. *Journal of Economic and Administrative Sciences, 34(2),* 109-111.

Kumar, V., & Das, S. (2017). Cost-benefit analysis of cloud computing with various deployment models. *Journal of Information Technology Management, 28(4),* 21-32.

Krämer, R. (2019). Change management for IT service management based on ITIL 4. *IT Professional, 21(4),* 42-48.

Langabeer II, J. R. (2018). *Healthcare operations management.* Jones & Bartlett Learning.

Mahadevan, B. (2019). Cross-functional collaboration in new product development: A network perspective on turnover. *Journal of Marketing, 83(2),* 64-86.

Marston, S., Li, Z., Bandyopadhyay, S., Zhang, J., & Ghalsasi, A. (2011). Cloud computing — The business perspective. *Decision Support Systems, 51(1),* 176-189.

Pinto, J. K. (2020). *Project management: Achieving competitive advantage.* Pearson.

Sánchez, A. M., Medina-López, C., & Romero, I. (2019). Lean, agile, resilient and green supply chain: A review. *Journal of Cleaner Production, 207,* 77-88.

Schöttle, J., & Duller, C. (2020). Sustainable procurement: Impact of procurement strategies on economic and ecological performance. *Journal of Purchasing and Supply Management, 26(2),* 100619.

Schwalbe, K. (2020). *Information technology project management.* Cengage Learning.

Sharma, S. K., & Mishra, P. (2021). Green IT practices: An analysis of benefits, challenges, and *environmental impacts. Journal of Cleaner Production, 280, 124474.*

Van Grembergen, W., De Haes, S., & Guldentops, E. (2019). Strategies for information technology governance. Routledge.

Weill, P., & Broadbent, M. (2019). Leveraging the new infrastructure: How market leaders capitalize on information technology. Harvard Business Press.

Zhang, Y., Sarker, S., & Basu, S. (2017). Exploring the links between the Toyota way and agility: A systematic literature review. International Journal of Production Economics, 193, 472-491.

Rachael Evans MA, FCMI

3. Financial Management Competencies for Non-Financial Managers

This paper discusses the critical role non-financial managers play in an organisation's financial management providing an overview of the key financial management concepts including Profit & Loss Statements, Balance Sheets, Financial Forecasting, Budgeting, and Strategic Financial Management. Each section discusses what non-financial managers should look for, how they perform basic tasks and introduces related basic formulas where applicable. Practical examples accompany each concept to illustrate their real-world application.

Introduction

The complexity and competitiveness of the contemporary business landscape necessitate a broader skill set for managers, extending beyond their core functional knowledge. An essential part of this skill set is understanding and applying financial management principles. Non-financial managers often find themselves involved in decisions that carry significant financial implications. Whether it's formulating and implementing strategic plans, executing marketing campaigns, or managing human resources, almost every decision within an organisation impacts its financial health. Therefore, it's critical for non-financial managers to comprehend the basic tenets of financial management to make informed and efficient business decisions (Brigham & Ehrhardt, 2013).

The primary aim of this paper is to elucidate the key financial management competencies that non-financial managers should possess, focusing on understanding Profit & Loss (P&L) statements, the Balance Sheet, Forecasting, Budgeting, and strategic financial management.

The insights and guidelines presented in this paper will empower non-financial managers with the necessary tools and understanding to contribute effectively to their organisation's profitability, financial health, and overall strategic objectives. It aims to bridge the gap between financial and non-financial managers, fostering an environment of comprehensive and collaborative decision-making, and ultimately driving business success.

From a personal perspective, I have seen how a comprehensive understanding of financial management can significantly enhance non-financial managers' decision-making abilities, strategic contributions, and overall effectiveness in their roles. This paper is therefore a consolidation of these insights and an effort to help non-financial managers navigate the seemingly complex world of financial management. Through this work, I hope to highlight the importance of these core financial competencies, demonstrating that they are not only beneficial but essential for non-financial managers in today's business environment.

For ease of use, each section has been broken down into components that should help you to navigate through the content. The Introduction: This provides a concise overview to familiarise you with the core concepts. Key Terms to Note: In this part, you'll find commonly used terminology, each accompanied by a succinct explanation to help you grasp its meaning and relevance. Fundamental Tasks and Formulas: This segment presents the essential tasks you'll encounter and the formulas you're likely to employ in financial management. Practical Application: An illustration of real-world usage of the concepts and formulas discussed, providing a concrete example to enhance understanding.

For ease of use, each section has been broken down into components that should help you to navigate through the content.

Introduction: This provides a concise overview to familiarise you with the core concepts.

Key Terms to Note: In this part, you'll find commonly used terminology, each accompanied by a succinct explanation to help you grasp its meaning and relevance.

Fundamental Tasks and Formulas: This segment presents the essential tasks you'll encounter and the formulas you're likely to employ in financial management.

Practical Application: An illustration of real-world usage of the concepts and formulas discussed, providing a concrete example to enhance understanding.

Understanding the Profit & Loss Statement (P&L)

Introduction

The Profit & Loss Statement, also referred to as the Income Statement, is a crucial financial report that encapsulates an organisation's revenues, costs, and expenses over a specified timeframe—typically a fiscal quarter or year. The main objective of this statement is to illustrate the company's profitability during the period under review (Anthony & Breitner, 2003).

Non-financial managers must comprehend how to read and interpret a P&L statement to gain an understanding of the organisation's financial performance. This knowledge equips managers to make data-driven decisions that can optimise profits and contribute to the organisation's overall financial health.

Key Terms to Note

Key metrics to focus on in a P&L statement include:

Gross Profit Margin: This indicates the total sales revenue after accounting for the cost of goods sold (COGS). It reflects the efficiency of an organisation's production process.

Operating Margin: This represents the profit a company makes on a dollar of sales after paying for variable costs of production, such as wages and raw materials, but before paying interest or tax.

Net Profit Margin: This is what remains of the income after all costs, taxes, and interest, have been deducted. It is the actual profit and a good indicator of the company's profitability.

These margins provide insights into the organisation's cost efficiency, operational efficiency, and overall profitability, respectively.

Fundamental Tasks and Formulas

To calculate these metrics, managers can use the following formulas:

- Gross Profit Margin = (Gross Profit / Revenue) * 100
- Operating Profit Margin = (Operating Profit / Revenue) * 100
- Net Profit Margin = (Net Profit / Revenue) * 100

Practical Application

Consider a company, 'ABC Ltd.' that generated revenue of £500,000 in a fiscal year. Its cost of goods sold is £200,000, and it has operational expenses of £150,000. After accounting for taxes and interest, the net income stands at £100,000.

- Gross Profit Margin = ((500,000 - 200,000) / 500,000) * 100 = 60%
- Operating Profit Margin = ((500,000 - 200,000 - 150,000) / 500,000) * 100 = 30%
- Net Profit Margin = (100,000 / 500,000) * 100 = 20%

Understanding these metrics allows a manager to gain insights into the profitability and efficiency of the company's operations, aiding strategic decision-making.

3. Financial Management Competencies

The Balance Sheet

Introduction

A Balance Sheet is a financial statement that presents a snapshot of an organisation's financial condition at a particular point in time. It provides a structured breakdown of the organisation's assets, liabilities, and shareholders' equity, effectively displaying what the organisation owns and owes, along with the investment made by shareholders (Parrino, Kidwell, & Bates, 2011).

Non-financial managers need to understand how to interpret a Balance Sheet to evaluate the organisation's financial health and sustainability. It empowers them to make informed decisions that can contribute towards maintaining financial stability and growth.

Key Terms to Note

Non-financial managers should focus on the following key indicators:

Current Ratio: This liquidity ratio indicates the company's ability to meet its short-term liabilities with its short-term assets. A higher current ratio implies greater short-term financial health.

Debt to Equity Ratio: This solvency ratio depicts how the organisation is financing its growth and how effectively it is using shareholders' equity. A high debt-to-equity ratio might indicate that the company has been aggressive in financing its growth with debt, which could pose risks.

Asset Turnover: This efficiency ratio shows how efficiently the organisation is using its assets to generate revenue.

Fundamental Tasks and Formulas

To calculate these ratios, managers can use the following formulas: •

- Current Ratio = Current Assets / Current Liabilities
- Debt to Equity Ratio = Total Debt / Total Equity
- Asset Turnover = Revenue / Average Total Assets

Practical Application

Let's consider a company, 'XYZ Ltd.' that has current assets worth £200,000 and current liabilities of £150,000. The total debt is £400,000, and the total equity is £350,000. The company has generated a revenue of £500,000 and the average total assets for the fiscal year stand at £600,000.

- Current Ratio = 200,000 / 150,000 = 1.33
- Debt to Equity Ratio = 400,000 / 350,000 = 1.14
- Asset Turnover = 500,000 / 600,000 = 0.83

In this scenario, the Current Ratio of 1.33 suggests that the company is in a healthy position to cover its short-term liabilities with its short-term assets. The Debt-to-Equity Ratio of 1.14 signifies that the company has more debt than equity, implying a relatively high-risk financial structure. The Asset Turnover of 0.83 indicates that the company generates 83 pence in sales for every pound invested in assets, a potential area for efficiency improvement. This understanding supports non-financial managers in making strategic decisions to drive financial stability and growth.

Forecasting

Introduction

Financial forecasting is the process of estimating future financial outcomes for an organisation based on historical data, market research, and economic trends. It is an integral part of financial planning and helps managers anticipate future financial conditions, facilitating strategic decision-making (Epstein & Lee, 2004).

Non-financial managers should understand the basics of financial forecasting to make proactive, informed business decisions. Being able to anticipate potential financial scenarios allows managers to plan more effectively and mitigate potential risks.

Key Terms to Note

When forecasting, managers should focus on the following:

Trends and Patterns: By observing historical data, managers can identify trends and patterns that may continue.

Impact of Internal and External Factors: Understanding how internal factors (like operational efficiency) and external factors (like economic conditions) affect financial performance can help refine forecasts.

3. Financial Management Competencies

Accuracy of Previous Forecasts: Comparing actual outcomes with previous forecasts can provide insights into how to improve future forecasts. If assumptions are used and/ or variance allowed for, it helps to show figures as a +/- range i.e., +/- 20% indicating that there is an expected variance of 20% above or below the provided figure.

Fundamental Tasks and Formulas

Forecasting involves several statistical techniques such as:

- Time Series Analysis: This uses historical data to predict future performance. For instance, if sales have grown by 10% annually for the past five years, it might be reasonable to predict a similar growth rate for the next year.

- Regression Analysis: This determines the relationship between different variables. For example, a company might forecast sales based on its marketing spend, assuming a consistent correlation between these two variables.

- Financial Modelling: This involves creating an abstract representation of a financial decision-making situation. For instance, managers might build a model to predict the impact of a new project on future cash flows.

Practical Application

Consider 'DEF Ltd.' it has grown its sales by 5% annually for the past five years, and it plans to increase its marketing spend by 20% next year. Suppose historical data shows a positive correlation between sales and marketing spend.

Using Time Series Analysis, if the sales this year were £500,000, the projected sales for next year would be £525,000 (£500,000 * 1.05).

Using Regression Analysis, if a 10% increase in marketing spend generally leads to a 2% increase in sales, a 20% increase in marketing spend might lead to an approximate 4% increase in sales. This equates to an additional £20,000 (£500,000 * 0.04), raising the forecasted sales to £545,000 (£525,000 + £20,000).

This example illustrates how non-financial managers can use forecasting tools to anticipate financial outcomes and support strategic planning.

Budgeting

Introduction

Budgeting is the process of creating a plan to spend an organisation's resources, providing a detailed roadmap of income and expenses over a specific period. It plays a pivotal role in financial planning, cost control, and performance evaluation (Hansen, Mowen, & Guan, 2009).

Non-financial managers should understand the principles of budgeting to manage their departmental resources efficiently, control costs, and contribute to the organisation's financial performance and strategic objectives.

Key Terms to Note

When setting a budget, managers should consider the following:

Historical Data: Previous years' revenues and expenses can provide a basis for predicting future budgetary figures.

Strategic Goals: The organisation's strategic goals should align with the budget. For instance, if the goal is to expand operations, the budget should reflect higher capital expenditure.

Cash Flow: A budget should consider the cash inflow and outflow to ensure the organisation maintains adequate liquidity to meet its obligations.

Fundamental Tasks and Formulas

The budgeting process typically involves the following steps:

- Determine expected income and expenses based on historical data and forecasting.
- Allocate resources to different departments or projects based on strategic priorities.
- Monitor the budget over time, compare actual results with budgeted figures, and adjust as needed.

There is no universal formula for creating a budget because it is tailored to each organisation's unique financial circumstances and strategic goals. However, the formula to calculate budget variance, which shows the difference between budgeted and actual figures, is as follows:

Budget Variance = Budgeted Amount - Actual Amount

Practical Application

Consider an organisation, 'GHI Ltd.', which set a budget for marketing expenses at £200,000 for the fiscal year. At the end of the year, the actual marketing expenses amounted to £210,000.

The budget variance in this case is: £200,000 (budgeted amount) - £210,000 (actual amount) = -£10,000

The negative variance indicates that actual expenses were higher than budgeted, suggesting that the company spent more on marketing than planned. This understanding can guide nonfinancial managers in planning and controlling future budgets to align with the organisation's financial objectives.

Strategy in Financial Management

Introduction

Strategic financial management involves the identification of financial goals, strategies to achieve these goals, and resources required to execute these strategies. It ensures that the organisation's financial resources are optimally utilised to achieve its long-term objectives (Brigham & Ehrhardt, 2013).

Non-financial managers should understand strategic financial management to make decisions that align with the organisation's financial strategy, thus contributing to its long-term growth and sustainability.

Key Terms to Note

When considering strategy in financial management, managers should pay attention to the following:

Alignment with Organisational Goals: The financial strategy should align with the overall organisational goals. For instance, if the goal is to expand, the financial strategy might involve securing funds for this expansion through equity or debt.

Risk and Return: Every financial decision involves a trade-off between risk and return. Managers need to assess the potential risk and expected return of financial decisions to ensure they contribute to the organisation's financial stability and growth.

Sustainability: The financial strategy should ensure the organisation's long-term financial health. This might involve maintaining a balanced mix of debt and equity or building a sufficient cash reserve to withstand economic downturns.

Fundamental Tasks and Formulas

Strategic financial management involves the following tasks:

- Defining long-term financial goals: These might involve increasing shareholder value, expanding the business, or improving profitability.
- Developing financial strategies: Based on the goals, managers develop strategies such as investing in new projects, acquiring other businesses, or issuing shares or bonds.
- Allocating resources: Managers allocate resources to implement these strategies, ensuring the most efficient use of the organisation's financial resources.

Financial formulas used in strategic decisions include calculations for Return on Investment (ROI), Net Present Value (NPV), and Internal Rate of Return (IRR).

Practical Application

Consider another organisation, 'JKL Ltd.', planning to invest in a new project that requires an initial investment of £1,000,000 and is expected to generate net cash inflows of £300,000 per year for the next 5 years.

The ROI can be calculated as follows:

ROI = (Total Net Returns / Total Investment) * 100

If JKL Ltd. expects £300,000 in net returns annually for 5 years, the total net returns would be £1,500,000. So, the ROI would be (1,500,000 / 1,000,000) * 100 = 150%

This calculation helps managers assess the effectiveness of the investment and decide whether it aligns with the organisation's financial strategy and goals.

Net Present Value (NPV)

Example The Net Present Value (NPV) is a financial metric widely used in capital budgeting and investment planning. NPV measures the profitability of a project by calculating the present values of cash inflows and outflows over a period, using a specified discount rate. If the NPV of a project is positive, it is considered profitable; if it's negative, the project is likely not profitable (Brealey, Myers, & Allen, 2011).

Now 'JKL Ltd.', is planning to invest in a new project that requires an initial investment of £1,000,000 and is expected to generate net cash inflows of £300,000 per year for the next 5 years. Assume the discount rate to be 10%.

The formula for NPV is:

NPV = $\sum$ [Cash inflow for the year / (1 + discount rate) ^ year] - Initial investment

The cash inflow is expected to be £300,000 each year for the next 5 years. The calculation for each year's cash inflow discounted back to present value at a rate of 10% would be as follows:

Year 1: £300,000 / (1+0.1) ^ 1 = £272,727 Year 2: £300,000 / (1+0.1) ^ 2 = £247,933 Year 3: £300,000 / (1+0.1) ^ 3 = £225,393 Year 4: £300,000 / (1+0.1) ^ 4 = £204,902 Year 5: £300,000 / (1+0.1) ^ 5 = £186,276

The total present value of inflows is the sum of these, which equals £1,137,231. The initial investment was £1,000,000.

Thus, the NPV of the project would be:

NPV = £1,137,231 - £1,000,000 = £137,231

Since the NPV is positive, this suggests that the project is expected to generate more profit than the cost of the initial investment, adjusted for the time value of money. This positive NPV indicates that the project could be a good investment, aligning with the organisation's financial strategy and goals.

Conclusion

The responsibility of effective financial management extends beyond the finance department and should be a core competency of all managers, regardless of their primary area of expertise. Understanding the basic principles of Profit & Loss Statements, Balance Sheets, Financial Forecasting, Budgeting, and Strategic Financial Management is critical for nonfinancial managers to contribute effectively to their organisation's financial health and strategic objectives.

Profit & Loss statements and Balance Sheets provide key insights into the organisation's financial performance and position. They highlight areas of strength and potential weaknesses that could impact financial stability and growth. Non-financial managers can use these financial statements to understand their department's contribution to the organisation's financial performance and to make informed decisions.

Financial Forecasting and Budgeting, meanwhile, are essential tools for planning and control. They enable managers to anticipate future financial conditions, plan resource allocation, and control costs effectively. By understanding and applying these tools, non-financial managers can contribute to the financial sustainability and growth of their organisations.

An understanding of Strategy in Financial Management allows non-financial managers to align their decisions with the organisation's financial strategy and goals. They can evaluate the financial implications of their decisions and ensure that they contribute to the organisation's long-term growth and sustainability.

By integrating these core financial competencies into their decision-making processes, nonfinancial managers can contribute significantly to enhancing the financial performance of their organisations, driving growth, and creating value. As the business landscape becomes increasingly complex and competitive, the role of non-financial managers in financial management will undoubtedly continue to grow in importance. Therefore, it is vital for nonfinancial managers to continuously develop their understanding of these principles and their application in real-world scenarios.

References

Anthony, R. N., & Breitner, L. (2003). *Core Concepts of Accounting Information Systems*. John Wiley & Sons.

Brealey, R. A., Myers, S. C., & Allen, F. (2011). *Principles of Corporate Finance*. McGrawHill/Irwin.

Brigham, E. F., & Ehrhardt, M. C. (2013). *Financial Management: Theory and Practice*. Cengage Learning.

Epstein, M. J., & Lee, J. Y. (2004). Implementing corporate strategy: From Tableaux de Bord to balanced scorecards. *European Management Journal, 22(2)*, 223-236.

Hansen, D. R., Mowen, M. M., & Guan, L. (2009). *Cost Management: Accounting and Control*. Cengage Learning.

Parrino, R., Kidwell, D. S., & Bates, T. W. (2011). *Fundamentals of Corporate Finance*. John Wiley & Sons.

Krysten M. Bacan

4. Harnessing Smart Processes for Hard Savings in Small and Medium-Sized Businesses: A Review of the Literature and Case Studies

This paper reviews the academic literature and case studies on how small and medium-sized businesses (SMBs) can achieve hard savings through the implementation of smart processes. We focus on the benefits of leveraging technology, streamlining operations, and fostering continuous improvement. The paper synthesises evidence from various sources, providing a comprehensive understanding of the potential for cost reduction and increased profitability in SMBs.

Introduction

In today's socio-economic, challenging business environment, small and medium-sized businesses (SMBs) face the challenge of optimising operations and reducing costs to remain competitive and viable (OECD, 2018). An approach to achieving hard savings is the implementation of smart processes, which utilise technology and data-driven insights to streamline operations and improve efficiency (Porter & Heppelmann, 2014). Through the integration of advanced technologies such as artificial intelligence (AI), machine learning, and automation, along with data analytics, SMBs can transform their operations and drive cost savings (Bughin et al., 2017; Deloitte, 2015).

To achieve operational excellence, SMBs should consider adopting a combination of lean management principles, continuous improvement practices, and smart processes that leverage technology and data analytics. This holistic approach enables SMBs to identify and address inefficiencies, reduce waste, and improve overall performance. By embracing these strategies, SMBs can achieve significant cost savings, enhance their competitive position in the market, and ensure sustainable growth in an increasingly complex business landscape.

This paper reviews the relevant literature and case studies to identify strategies for harnessing smart processes in SMBs and to provide practical insights and recommendations for their successful implementation.

Technology-driven Efficiency

Various technologies have been demonstrated to significantly enhance efficiency and deliver hard savings for SMBs, helping them remain competitive and sustainable in an ever-changing market landscape (Bughin et al., 2017). These cutting-edge solutions not only optimize operations but also contribute to improved customer satisfaction, employee productivity, and overall business performance.

The following are key examples of such transformative technologies:

Robotic Process Automation (RPA): RPA automates repetitive, rule-based tasks, increasing efficiency, and reducing human error (Lacity & Willcocks, 2016). A case study by PwC (2018) highlights the successful implementation of RPA in a small insurance firm, resulting in a 50% reduction in operational costs. RPA can also improve accuracy, enhance compliance, and allow employees to focus on higher-value tasks, leading to increased overall productivity.

Cloud Computing: Cloud-based solutions enable SMBs to access powerful computing resources and software without significant upfront investments (Marston et al., 2011). This technology allows for greater scalability and flexibility, enabling businesses to quickly adapt to changing market conditions. A study by Kshetri (2013) found that SMBs that adopted cloud computing reported a 25% reduction in IT costs, as well as improvements in collaboration, data storage, and accessibility.

Data Analytics: Data-driven decision-making allows SMBs to optimize their operations and identify areas for cost reduction (LaValle et al., 2011). By analyzing large volumes of data, businesses can uncover hidden patterns, correlations, and insights that inform strategic decisions. A case study by Deloitte (2015) demonstrates how a small manufacturing firm used data

4. Harnessing Smart Processes for Hard Savings

analytics to identify inefficiencies in its supply chain, resulting in a 20% reduction in inventory costs. Additionally, data analytics can help SMBs enhance customer service, optimize marketing efforts, and improve overall business performance.

Internet of Things (IoT): IoT technologies connect physical devices, vehicles, and other items to the internet, enabling data collection, analysis, and remote monitoring (Gubbi et al., 2013). SMBs can leverage IoT to optimize resource utilization, monitor equipment performance, and predict maintenance needs. For example, a study by Accenture (2016) found that SMBs that adopted IoT solutions experienced a 30% reduction in maintenance costs and a 35% reduction in downtime.

By adopting these and other advanced technologies, SMBs can streamline their operations, increase efficiency, and deliver hard savings that contribute to their overall competitiveness and success in the marketplace.

Streamlining Operations

By streamlining operations, small and medium-sized businesses (SMBs) can reduce waste, improve productivity, and achieve hard savings (Radnor et al., 2012). One effective approach is the adoption of lean management principles, which can be applied to various aspects of an SMB's operations. Key areas include inventory management, where lean practices help minimise stock levels and eliminate excess inventory costs (Womack & Jones, 2003); process improvement, which involves identifying and eliminating non-value-added activities in workflows, thereby increasing operational efficiency (Liker, 2004); and workforce optimisation, where lean principles can help enhance employee productivity through skill development, cross-training, and efficient allocation of tasks (Womack & Jones, 2003).

Real-world examples demonstrate the success of implementing lean principles in SMBs. For instance, a study by Shah & Ward (2007) found that SMBs that adopted lean principles reported an average cost reduction of 15%.

In another case study, a small manufacturing company implemented lean practices to optimise their production process, resulting in a 25% reduction in lead time and a 20% increase in overall productivity (Tapping et al., 2002). These examples illustrate the potential benefits of streamlining operations using lean management principles, enabling SMBs to achieve significant hard savings and improve their competitive position in the market.

Continuous Improvement

Fostering a culture of continuous improvement is crucial for driving long-term hard savings for small and medium-sized businesses (SMBs) (Bessant et al., 2001). By consistently reviewing processes, identifying inefficiencies, and implementing improvements, SMBs can achieve incremental cost reductions over time, which ultimately contribute to their bottom line (Jurburg et al., 2017). This approach involves a commitment to regularly evaluating and refining all aspects of the business, from operations and supply chain management to customer service and employee engagement.

One notable example of a company that successfully embraced a continuous improvement culture is Toyota. In a case study by Toyota (2010), the company's commitment to continuous improvement, known as the "Toyota Production System" or "Kaizen," resulted ina 30% reduction in production costs over a five-year period. This impressive outcome was achieved through various initiatives, including process optimisation, waste elimination, employee empowerment, and ongoing skill development.

Other SMBs can learn from Toyota's example and adopt similar practices to drive long-term cost savings. By encouraging employees at all levels to contribute ideas for improvement and providing the necessary resources and support to implement these changes, SMBs can create an environment where continuous improvement thrives. In turn, this leads to increased operational efficiency, reduced waste, and sustained cost savings that contribute to the overall success and competitiveness of the business.

Final Thoughts

Small and medium-sized businesses (SMBs) must adapt and innovate in today's competitive business environment to optimize operations, reduce costs, and remain viable. By harnessing smart processes that integrate technology, data-driven insights, lean management principles, and continuous improvement practices, SMBs can transform their operations and achieve significant hard savings.

The integration of advanced technologies such as artificial intelligence, machine learning, automation, and data analytics enables SMBs to streamline operations, enhance decisionmaking, and improve overall performance. In addition, fostering a culture of continuous improvement empowers

4. Harnessing Smart Processes for Hard Savings

employees at all levels to contribute to the ongoing refinement and optimisation of business processes.

By embracing these strategies, SMBs can achieve long-term cost savings, strengthen their competitive position in the market, and ensure sustainable growth in an increasingly complex business landscape. As technology continues to advance and new opportunities emerge, it is essential for SMBs to remain agile and adaptable, leveraging these developments to drive further improvements and maintain a competitive edge.

Furthermore, SMBs should prioritise employee engagement and skill development to maximise the benefits of smart processes and continuous improvement initiatives. Providing ongoing training and support for staff ensures they are equipped with the necessary skills and knowledge to effectively contribute to the organisation's performance improvement efforts.

The combination of smart processes, continuous improvement practices, and a commitment to employee development will enable SMBs to achieve operational excellence, reduce costs, and remain competitive in an ever-evolving global economy. By proactively pursuing these strategies, SMBs can ensure their long-term success and resilience in the face of ongoing challenges and market disruptions.

References

Accenture. (2016). Winning with the Industrial Internet of Things. Accenture Strategy.

Bessant, J., Caffyn, S., & Gallagher, M. (2001). An evolutionary model of continuous improvement behavior. Technovation, 21(2), 67-77.

Bughin, J., Hazan, E., Ramaswamy, S., Chui, M., Allas, T., Dahlström, P., ... & Trench, M. (2017). Artificial intelligence: The next digital frontier?. McKinsey Global Institute.

Deloitte. (2015). Analytics in action: Breakthroughs and barriers on the journey to ROI. Deloitte University Press.

Gubbi, J., Buyya, R., Marusic, S., & Palaniswami, M. (2013). Internet of Things (IoT): A ision, architectural elements, and future directions. Future Generation Computer Systems, 29(7), 1645-1660.

Jurburg, D., Viles, E., Tanco, M., & Mateo, R. (2017). What are the key improvement areas in SMEs? An empirical research in Spanish firms. Total Quality Management & Business Excellence, 28(3-4), 246-265.

Kshetri, N. (2013). Privacy and security issues in cloud computing: The role of institutions and institutional evolution. *Telecommunications Policy, 37*(4-5), 372-386.

Lacity, M. C., & Willcocks, L. P. (2016). A new approach to automating services. *MIT Sloan Management Review, 58*(1), 40-49.

LaValle, S., Lesser, E., Shockley, R., Hopkins, M. S., & Kruschwitz, N. (2011). Big data, analytics and the path from insights to value. *MIT Sloan Management Review, 52*(2), 21-32.

Liker, J. K. (2004). *The Toyota way: 14 management principles from the world's greatest manufacturer.* McGraw-Hill.

Marston, S., Li, Z., Bandyopadhyay, S., Zhang, J., & Ghalsasi, A. (2011). Cloud computing—The business perspective. *Decision Support Systems, 51*(1), 176-189.

OECD. (2018). *Small, medium, strong. Trends in SME performance and business conditions.* OECD Publishing.

Porter, M. E., & Heppelmann, J. E. (2014). How smart, connected products are transforming competition. *Harvard Business Review, 92*(11), 64-88.

PwC. (2018). *Sizing the prize: What's the real value of AI for your business and how can you capitalize?* PwC Global AI Study.

Radnor, Z. J., Holweg, M., & Waring, J. (2012). Lean in healthcare: The unfilled promise? *Social Science & Medicine, 74*(3), 364-371.

Shah, R., & Ward, P. T. (2007). Defining and developing measures of lean production. *Journal of Operations Management, 25*(4), 785-805.

Tapping, D., Luyster, T., & Shuker, T. (2002). *Value stream management: Eight steps to planning, mapping, and sustaining lean improvements.* Productivity Press.

Toyota. (2010). *The Toyota Way.* Toyota Motor Corporation.

Womack, J. P., & Jones, D. T. (2003). *Lean thinking: Banish waste and create wealth in your corporation.* Simon and Schuster.

Rachael Evans MA, FCMI

5. The Innovation Gap: A Critical Analysis of UK and US Banking Technology

In this short paper, I will examine the factors contributing to the perceived lag in innovation within the UK and US banking sectors, focusing on the implications of poor management, incorrect interpretation of industry regulations, and over-reliance on external consultants. Through a review of relevant literature and case studies, I will further examine how inefficient decision making and lack of strategic vision, over-caution in interpreting regulations, and heavy reliance on external consultants can hinder banks from embracing novel technologies and improving their services. The consequences of this stagnation in innovation are far-reaching, including reduced competitiveness, limited financial services, and decreased profitability.

Addressing these challenges is essential for banks to maintain their pivotal role in the global economy and ensure they can continue to serve their customers effectively in an increasingly digital financial landscape. I conclude by offering recommendations for banks to foster a culture of innovation, improve their regulatory understanding, and strike a balance between internal expertise and external consulting services.

Introduction

The banking industry is a cornerstone of the global economy, for all its good and bad, and its ability to innovate and adopt new technologies significantly influences its sustainability, growth, and the range of services it can offer consumers. As technology rapidly evolves, consumer expectations for convenient, secure, and personalised financial services have increased. The industry's ability to meet these expectations depends on its capacity to innovate and leverage cutting-edge technologies.

The innovation gap in banking technology affects the industry's competitiveness and has significant implications for consumers. The slow adoption of new technologies restricts the availability of convenient and affordable financial services, which in turn limits consumers' access to credit, digital banking services, and personalised financial management tools. The failure to keep pace with innovation can disproportionately affect underserved communities, exacerbating financial inequality and potentially increasing the number of unbanked and underbanked individuals (Beck, Demirguc-Kunt, & Levine, 2007).

Concerns are growing about the capability of UK and US banks to keep pace with technological advancements, particularly compared to Asian counterparts such as China and Singapore (Chishti & Barberis, 2016). This article explores the hypothesis that UK and US banking technology has fallen behind due to a combination of poor management, misconstrued interpretation of industry regulation, and an over-reliance on costly consultants and proposes possible solutions to help UK and US banks address these challenges and maintain their pivotal role in the global economy.

Ineffective Management

Inefficient decision-making and a lack of a strategic vision can result in a sluggish adoption of novel technologies, ultimately affecting a bank's ability to meet consumer expectations and maintain a competitive edge (Ennew & Waite, 2013; Tushman & O'Reilly, 1996). Several factors contribute to this inefficiency, including resistance to change, inadequate communication, and misaligned incentives.

One prominent example is Citigroup's failed attempt to revamp its banking technology systems. The project, which aimed to modernise the bank's core infrastructure and streamline operations, faced numerous challenges. Unclear project objectives, lack of executive support, and miscommunication between different teams led to delays and cost overruns, ultimately resulting in a loss of nearly $500 million for the company (McGregor, 2010).

Similarly, Wells Fargo's delay in adopting mobile banking technologies can be attributed to its management's initial resistance to change. Executives at the bank were hesitant to embrace digital banking services, fearing that it might cannibalise their existing business and alienate customers who preferred traditional banking methods (Perez, 2016). This resistance to change prevented the bank from quickly capitalising on the growing demand for mobile banking services, allowing competitors to gain an advantage in the market.

A further issue that can impede innovation is misaligned incentives within the organisation. When performance metrics and rewards focus primarily on short-term financial gains, employees may be discouraged from pursuing innovative projects that require long-term investments and may not yield immediate results (Christensen, 1997). This can lead to a lack of support for innovation initiatives, ultimately hampering the organisation's ability to adapt to changing market conditions and consumer preferences.

To address these challenges, banks should establish clear strategic goals and create an organisational culture that encourages innovation and embraces change. This includes promoting open communication between teams, fostering a growth mindset, and designing incentive systems that reward innovative thinking and long-term value creation (Damanpour & Schneider, 2006). By addressing the underlying issues that contribute to inefficient decision-making and a lack of strategic vision, banks can accelerate their adoption of novel technologies and remain competitive in an increasingly digital financial landscape.

Misinterpreted Industry Regulation

Over-caution in interpreting banking regulations can stifle technological innovation and hinder banks' ability to adapt to changing market conditions and consumer preferences (Barker & Levine, 2015; Avgouleas & Kiayias, 2018). This overcaution often stems from a lack of understanding of the regulations, a conservative approach to risk management, or the fear of regulatory penalties.

A notable example of overcaution in interpreting regulations is the misinterpretation of the EU's General Data Protection Regulation (GDPR) by some banks. Instead of recognising the GDPR as a framework that promotes the responsible use of personal data, these banks erroneously viewed it as an absolute barrier to adopting certain fintech solutions, such as open banking initiatives and data-driven personalised services (Giannetti & Simonov, 2019). This misinterpretation not only limited the banks' ability to leverage new technologies but also constrained their capacity to offer improved financial services to consumers.

In the US, a similar issue arises with the interpretation of the Dodd-Frank Act, a regulatory reform that aimed to promote financial stability and protect consumers following the 2008 financial crisis. While the Dodd-Frank Act imposes certain restrictions on banks to reduce systemic risk, many banks overestimate these limitations, avoiding potential beneficial collaborations with fintech firms (Gomber, Koch, & Siering, 2017). This cautious approach hampers the ability of banks to adopt innovative technologies and business models that could enhance their competitiveness and provide better financial services to customers.

To overcome these challenges, banks should invest in comprehensive regulatory training and foster a culture of regulatory compliance that balances innovation and risk management. By engaging with regulators and participating in industry-wide dialogues, banks can gain a better understanding of the regulatory landscape and identify opportunities for innovation within the boundaries of the law (Höchle, Kranz, & Scorna, 2020). Additionally, banks should consider working with specialised legal and compliance advisors who can help navigate the complex regulatory environment and ensure that innovative projects align with regulatory requirements.

By adopting a more informed and balanced approach to interpreting banking regulations, banks can overcome the over-caution that stifles innovation and take advantage of emerging opportunities in the evolving financial services industry.

Over-Reliance on Expensive Consultants

Heavy reliance on external consultants can create a dependency that stifles innovation and strains resources, ultimately impacting a bank's ability to maintain competitiveness and serve its customers effectively (KPMG, 2020; Mathews, 2015). While consultants can provide valuable expertise and insights to drive transformation projects, an over-reliance on their services can hinder internal capabilities and divert resources from other strategic priorities.

A prime example of this issue is Deutsche Bank, which spent billions on external consulting services to drive its digital transformation initiatives. Despite this significant investment, the bank faced substantial challenges in integrating new technologies and realising the expected benefits from the transformation (Enrich, 2019). This case highlights the potential pitfalls of excessive reliance on external consultants, as it can lead to a lack of ownership and accountability within the organisation.

Another report by Accenture underscores the scale of this issue in the banking industry. According to the report, banks globally spent $1 trillion on consultants between 2008 and 2018, but only 37% of these projects yielded positive results (Accenture, 2019). This finding suggests that a more balanced approach to leveraging external expertise is necessary to optimise resources and achieve desired outcomes.

To address the challenges associated with over-reliance on external consultants, banks should focus on building internal capabilities and fostering a culture of continuous learning and innovation. This can be achieved through targeted investments in employee training, talent acquisition, and the creation of cross-functional teams that promote knowledge sharing and collaboration. Additionally, banks should develop a clear strategy for engaging with external consultants, ensuring that their expertise is used in a targeted and cost-effective manner that complements, rather than supplants, internal capabilities.

By striking a balance between internal expertise and external consulting services, banks can build a more sustainable foundation for innovation and digital transformation, ultimately enhancing their competitiveness and ability to serve customers in the rapidly evolving financial services landscape.

The Impact of Weak Innovation

The failure to keep pace with innovation has several implications for both the banking industry and consumers. These impacts range from reduced competitiveness to limited financial services and decreased profitability. A more detailed analysis of these implications is provided below:

1. **Reduced Competitiveness:** Banks that lag in technological advancements risk losing market share to more technologically advanced competitors, both domestic and international (Demirguc-Kunt & Levine, 2008; Chishti & Barberis, 2016). As technology driven financial services become more prevalent, customers are likely to shift their preferences towards banks that can offer seamless, user-friendly, and secure digital experiences. Additionally, traditional banks face increasing competition from fintech companies and digital banks that

are unburdened by legacy systems and are able to quickly adapt to new technologies (EY, 2019).

2. **Limited Financial Services:** Slow adoption of new technologies restricts the availability of convenient and affordable financial services, disproportionately affecting underserved communities (Beck, Demirguc-Kunt, & Levine, 2007; Claessens & Rojas-Suarez, 2020). By failing to leverage emerging technologies, such as mobile banking, digital lending, and AI-driven financial management tools, banks limit the range of services they can offer to customers. This not only restricts access to credit and financial services for underbanked populations but also exacerbates financial inequality and contributes to the persistence of the unbanked population (World Bank, 2018)

3. **Decreased Profitability:** Banks that fail to adopt cost-saving and revenue-generating technologies may see declining profits, threatening their long-term viability (Berger & Bouwman, 2013; Frame, Srinivasan, & Woosley, 2001). Innovative technologies, such as robotic process automation (RPA) and AI, can help banks streamline their operations, reduce costs, and improve efficiency (Deloitte, 2020). By not adopting these technologies, banks risk incurring higher operational costs and diminished profitability. Moreover, the inability to offer a wide range of digital financial services may result in reduced customer acquisition and retention, further impacting the banks' bottom line.

Ultimately, the failure to keep pace with innovation in the banking sector has far-reaching consequences, from reduced competitiveness to limited financial services and decreased profitability. Addressing these challenges is essential for banks to maintain their pivotal role in the global economy and ensure they can continue to serve their customers effectively in an increasingly digital financial landscape.

6. Conclusion & Recommendations

The capacity for innovation and the adoption of new technologies are critical factors in determining the success and competitiveness of the banking industry. UK and US banks must address the challenges posed by poor management, misconstrued interpretation of industry regulation, and an over-reliance on costly consultants to bridge the innovation gap. Doing so is essential for maintaining their competitiveness and has far-reaching implications for consumers, who increasingly demand convenient, secure, and personalised financial services.

In addition to the strategies discussed earlier, there are several other recommendations that can help UK and US banks accelerate innovation and maintain their competitiveness in the global financial landscape. These recommendations focus on fostering collaboration with fintech companies, embracing emerging technologies, and promoting financial inclusion. By implementing these strategies, banks can not only enhance their ability to innovate but also improve the range of financial services available to consumers, ultimately contributing to the overall stability and growth of the financial sector.

1. **Strengthening Collaboration and Partnerships:** Banks should proactively seek partnerships with fintech companies and other financial institutions to leverage their technological expertise, innovative business models, and access to new customer segments (Chishti & Barberis, 2016). By collaborating with these entities, banks can accelerate the development and deployment of innovative solutions and stay ahead of the competition.

2. **Investing in Emerging Technologies**: Banks should actively explore and invest in emerging technologies such as artificial intelligence, blockchain, and big data analytics to enhance their operational efficiency, improve customer experience, and create new revenue streams (Deloitte, 2020). By staying up to date with technological advancements, banks can identify and capitalise on opportunities for innovation.

3. **Promoting a Culture of Experimentation:** To foster innovation, banks should encourage a culture of experimentation and learning, allowing employees to test new ideas and learn from failures (Damanpour & Schneider, 2006). This approach can help banks identify promising innovations, refine them, and scale them across the organisation.

4. Establishing Innovation Labs: Banks should consider setting up dedicated innovation labs or centres of excellence to incubate, develop, and test new ideas, technologies, and business models (EY, 2019). These labs can serve as hubs for innovation, enabling banks to stay at the cutting edge of technological advancements and drive digital transformation initiatives.

5. Enhancing Cybersecurity Measures: As banks adopt new technologies and digital services, they must also strengthen their cybersecurity measures to protect customer data and maintain trust (World Economic Forum, 2018). By investing in robust cybersecurity infrastructure, banks can safeguard their customers and ensure the continued growth of digital financial services.

To foster innovation and sustain competitiveness, UK and US banks should invest in strong leadership, develop a clear strategic vision, and cultivate a culture of innovation within their organisations. They must also enhance their understanding of the regulatory landscape and find ways to reduce dependency on expensive consultants. By leveraging collaboration with fintech companies and embracing new technological advancements, banks can better serve their customers and create more inclusive financial ecosystems.

Addressing these challenges will help banks maintain their position at the forefront of technological innovation, ensuring they continue to play a vital role in the global economy. Furthermore, by fostering innovation, banks can expand the range of services available to consumers, improve financial inclusion, and contribute to the overall stability and growth of the financial sector.

References

Accenture. (2019). *Banking Technology Vision 2019*. Accenture.

Avgouleas, E., & Kiayias, A. (2018). The promise and perils of blockchain technology in financial services: A risk-based approach. *International Review of Financial Analysis, 62*, 110-125.

Beck, T., Demirguc-Kunt, A., & Levine, R. (2007). Finance, inequality and the poor. *Journal of Economic Growth, 12(1)*, 27-49.

Berger, A. N., & Bouwman, C. H. (2013). How does capital affect bank performance during financial crises? *Journal of Financial Economics, 109(1)*, 146-176.

Chishti, S., & Barberis, J. (2016). *The Fintech Book: The Financial Technology Handbook for Investors, Entrepreneurs and Visionaries*. John Wiley & Sons.

Christensen, C. M. (1997). *The Innovator's Dilemma: When New Technologies Cause Great Firms to Fail*. Harvard Business School Press.

Claessens, S., & Rojas-Suarez, L. (2020). *Financial Regulations for Improving Financial Inclusion*. Center for Global Development.

Damanpour, F., & Schneider, M. (2006). Phases of the adoption of innovation in organizations: Effects of the environment, organization, and top managers. British Journal of Management, 17 (3), 215-236.

Deloitte. (2020). The future of banking: A time to reimagine, transform, and thrive. Deloitte.

Deloitte. (2020). Banking Industry Outlook: Banking reimagined. Retrieved from https://www2.deloitte.com/us/en/insights/industry/financial-services/banking-industryoutlook. html

Demirguc-Kunt, A., & Levine, R. (2008). Finance, Financial Sector Policies, and Long-Run Growth. World Bank Policy Research Working Paper No. 4469.

Ennew, C., & Waite, N. (2013). Financial Services Marketing: An International Guide to Principles and Practice. Routledge.

Enrich, D. (2019). Dark Towers: Deutsche Bank, Donald Trump, and an Epic Trail of Destruction. HarperCollins.

EY. (2019). Global FinTech Adoption Index 2019. Retrieved from https://assets.ey.com/content/dam/ey-sites/ey-com/en_gl/topics/banking-capital-markets/eyglobal-fintech-adoption-index.pdf

Frame, W. S., Srinivasan, A., & Woosley, L. (2001). The effect of credit scoring on small business lending. Journal of Money, Credit, and Banking, 33(3), 813-825.

Giannetti, M., & Simonov, A. (2019). Financial regulation and innovation: The role of the GDPR in the fintech industry. Journal of Financial Stability, 42, 100708.

Gomber, P., Koch, J. A., & Siering, M. (2017). Digital Finance and FinTech: Current research and future research directions. Journal of Business Economics, 87(5), 537-580.

Höchle, D., Kranz, J., & Scorna, U. (2020). Innovation regulation in the financial industry: Balancing between market protection and market fostering. Journal of Business Economics, 90 (1), 97-124.

KPMG. (2020). The future of consulting in financial services. KPMG.

Mathews, S. (2015). The hidden costs of external consulting. McKinsey Quarterly, 3, 104-107.

McGregor, R. (2010). Citigroup's failed attempt to redesign its banking systems cost it hundreds of millions of dollars. Financial Times.

Perez, S. (2016). How Wells Fargo went from bank laggard to a leader in mobile banking. Forbes.

Tushman, M. L., & O'Reilly, C. A. (1996). Ambidextrous organizations: Managing evolutionary and revolutionary change. California Management Review, 38(4), 8-30.

World Economic Forum. (2018). Innovation in Financial Services: A dynamic new approach for identifying and scaling breakthrough ideas. Retrieved from https://www.weforum.org/whitepapers/innovation-in-financial-services-a-dynamic-newapproach-for-identifying-and-scaling-breakthrough-ideas

Rachael Evans MA, FCMI

6. The Hidden Cost of Saving: Unravelling the Impact of Underinvestment in Technology in the UK

This article explores the focus on cost-minimization in technology investment within the UK and how this financial management-centric perspective influences productivity, staff satisfaction, and growth. The UK's bias towards financial control has shaped the investment landscape, often prioritizing short-term savings over the long-term strategic advantages conferred by technology. Despite the critical role technology plays in today's digital economy, underinvestment persists due to prevailing financial management ideologies.

Comparisons with other developed nations indicate that countries investing more strategically in technology enjoy increased productivity and competitiveness. I will illustrate that a lack of adequate technology investment leads to reduced productivity, declining staff satisfaction due to antiquated or inefficient systems, and ultimately, stunted growth.

The article presents cases from firms such as Google and Kodak, illustrating the possible positive and negative impacts of technology investment on growth. It then outlines the imperative for change within the UK business context, suggesting a shift from viewing technology as an expense to recognizing it as a strategic tool for growth. This transition involves strategic planning, investing in infrastructure and skills, partnerships, and leadership commitment. Although the process may take several years, the potential benefits make it a crucial step for the UK's future competitiveness.

I conclude by summarising that a refocus on strategic technology investment is a pivotal factor in enhancing productivity, improving staff satisfaction, and driving growth, thus ensuring UK businesses remain competitive in the increasingly digital global economy.

Cost Minimization in Technology Investment, an Introduction

Given the pace of technological change and the reliance upon computing and innovation, it is a widely accepted key driver of economic growth and competitiveness. Indeed, a wealth of research has demonstrated that strategic investment in technology can enhance productivity, stimulate innovation, improve customer satisfaction, and positively impact overall business performance (Brynjolfsson and Hitt, 2000; Mithas et al., 2011).

Despite this, the UK seems to lag in leveraging the benefits of technology due to an approach that focuses primarily on cost minimization rather than strategic technology investment. This approach, largely influenced by a financial management perspective, can limit organizations' ability to fully exploit the potential benefits of technological advancements.

A tendency to prioritize short-term cost savings over long-term strategic investments is often driven by a focus on achieving immediate financial results, whether it's boosting quarterly earnings or meeting budget targets. However, this approach can have unintended consequences that are detrimental to the health and sustainability of the economy.

The overreliance on financial management at the expense of strategic technology investment can lead to underperformance in several key areas, including productivity, staff satisfaction, and overall economic growth. Furthermore, the lack of appropriate technology investment can stifle innovation, hamper the delivery of quality services, and create a gap between the UK and other developed nations that prioritize and effectively manage technology investments.

Therefore, it is crucial to scrutinize this issue, as understanding the impacts of cost minimization in technology investment can inform better policy and management practices. This, in turn, could help shift the UK's approach towards a more balanced one, where financial management is still important but does not stifle technological advancement and innovation.

Impact on Productivity

A lack of technology investment can significantly hamper productivity, resulting in inefficiencies, delays, and limitations in a firm's capacity to innovate. When companies fail to leverage new technologies, they miss out on opportunities to automate processes, optimize their operations, and remain competitive in a rapidly evolving marketplace.

For example, the UK construction industry has been cited as one that suffers from significant productivity issues. A report from McKinsey Global Institute (2017) pointed out that the construction sector's productivity has barely increased over the past 20 years. Compared to other sectors such as manufacturing, which has seen substantial productivity gains due to automation and technology investment, the construction sector's lack of digitization and reliance on traditional methods have contributed to its stagnant productivity.

This lack of technology investment not only affects individual sectors but also has broader implications for the UK economy. According to the Office for National Statistics (ONS), the UK's productivity growth has been slow for over a decade since the financial crisis of 2008, with productivity in 2018 being only slightly higher than its pre-downturn peak in 2007. This is in stark contrast with other G7 countries like the United States and Germany, which have seen stronger productivity growth over the same period (ONS, 2018).

Looking at specific areas, one clear place where technology investment can boost productivity is in automating routine tasks. For instance, the retail industry could increase productivity by implementing automated inventory management systems, freeing up workers to focus on customer service and other higher-value tasks. Similarly, the healthcare sector could benefit from electronic medical records and telemedicine, which can streamline processes and improve service delivery.

Ultimately, underinvestment in technology could lead to stagnated productivity growth, which in turn affects the overall competitiveness and potential for economic growth. Investing in digital transformation is thus critical to boost productivity and drive economic growth in the long run.

Impact on Staff Satisfaction

There's a growing body of research suggesting a strong correlation between technology investment, staff satisfaction, and productivity. Modern technologies not only automate routine tasks, thereby reducing workload, but also provide employees with tools that can make their work more engaging, flexible, and efficient.

In a digital economy, employees increasingly expect their workplace technology to match the convenience and usability of the technology they use in their personal lives. When organizations fail to meet these expectations, it can lead to employee frustration, decreased job satisfaction, and lower productivity.

For example, poor investment in technology could mean outdated systems that are slow, prone to crashes, or simply inefficient. Employees forced to work with such systems may experience higher levels of stress, frustration, and job dissatisfaction, leading to lower overall productivity. A study by Unisys found that employees who have access to the technology they need to do their job effectively are 51% more likely to be satisfied at work (Unisys, 2019).

Inadequate technology investment can also contribute to high staff turnover rates. Dissatisfied employees are more likely to look for new job opportunities, and the costs associated with employee turnover can be substantial. These include the direct costs of hiring and training new employees, as well as indirect costs such as lost productivity during the transition period, reduced morale among remaining staff, and the potential impact on customer service and reputation. According to the Society for Human Resource Management (SHRM), the total cost of replacing an employee can range from tens of thousands of dollars to 1.5-2 times an employee's annual salary (SHRM, 2016).

Furthermore, the ability to attract and retain top talent can be affected by an organization's technological standing. Prospective employees, particularly those in tech-savvy younger generations, may view a company's technology investment as a reflection of its overall innovation and growth potential. If a company is seen as technologically backwards, it may struggle to attract and retain the skilled workers necessary for success in the digital economy.

6. The Hidden Cost of Saving

Technology investment plays a vital role in staff satisfaction, productivity, and retention. Neglecting this investment can lead to a myriad of negative effects, from reduced productivity to high staff turnover, which can significantly impact a company's financial performance and competitive standing.

Impact on Growth

Investing in technology has significant implications for an organization's growth trajectory. A robust technology strategy can facilitate expansion, streamline operations, enhance innovation, and improve competitiveness. Conversely, a failure to invest in technology can lead to stagnation and business decline.

The Positive Impact

A study by Brynjolfsson and Hitt (2003) demonstrated a significant positive relationship between IT investment and productivity, a key driver of economic growth. The researchers found that firms investing in technology saw an output elasticity of around 0.5 – that is, a 10% increase in technology capital resulted in approximately a 5% increase in output.

A good example of this is the global tech company, Google. Google has consistently invested heavily in technology and innovation – in 2020 alone, the company spent over $26 billion on research and development (R&D) (Statista, 2021). This relentless focus on technology has led to the development of new products and services, from its pioneering search engine to its cloud computing services, fuelling Google's exponential growth.

The Negative Impact

On the flip side, a lack of technology investment can hinder growth. A classic example is Kodak, once a giant in the film photography industry. Despite inventing the first digital camera in 1975, Kodak was slow to invest in this new technology, choosing to focus on its existing film-based business instead. This failure to adapt and invest in digital technology ultimately led to Kodak's bankruptcy in 2012 (Economist, 2012).

Research by Polder et al. (2010) supports this anecdotal evidence, showing that firms that fail to invest in innovation display slower growth rates compared to their more innovative counterparts.

Organizations that strategically invest in technology tend to outperform their peers in terms of productivity and growth, whereas those who fail to do so often lag. It's clear that in the digital age, technology investment should be a key consideration for any organization aiming to thrive and expand.

The UK's Emphasis on Financial Management

The UK's focus on financial management can be traced back to the historical and ideological influences shaping its economic and political institutions. In the late 20th century, the UK, under the leadership of Prime Minister Margaret Thatcher, began adopting neoliberal economic principles. This included an emphasis on fiscal austerity, deregulation, privatization, and a reduction in government spending. These policies reflect a belief in the power of market mechanisms to drive economic growth and efficiency.

Despite the adverse long-term effects that this strategy might have, several reasons can explain why the UK continues to operate under this model.

1. Political ideology: Neoliberal thinking, with its emphasis on economic freedom and deregulation, remains influential in many political circles. This ideology often favours austerity and fiscal discipline, arguing that these policies can stimulate economic growth by creating a more favourable environment for private sector investment.

2. Short-termism: Political and business leaders often face pressure to deliver quick, tangible results. For politicians, this can be driven by electoral cycles. For business leaders, there might be pressure from shareholders for short-term financial gains. This can result in an emphasis on cost-cutting and financial efficiency, at the expense of longer-term, strategic investments such as technology.

3. Financial sector dominance: The UK, particularly London, is a global hub for the financial sector. The power and influence of this sector can drive a greater emphasis on financial indicators of success, such as profitability and return on investment, over other factors such as long-term growth or worker satisfaction.

The reasons to move away from an overly finance-focused model are multiple:

1. Balanced growth: While financial management is an important aspect of any economy, an overemphasis on cost-cutting and short-term profitability can lead to underinvestment in areas crucial for long-term growth, such as technology, infrastructure, and human capital.

6. The Hidden Cost of Saving

2. Societal well-being: Economic policy should not solely focus on financial indicators but also consider broader measures of societal well-being. Overemphasis on fiscal austerity can lead to underfunding of public services, rising inequality, and lower overall life satisfaction.
3. Resilience: Economies that are overly dependent on one sector, such as finance, are more vulnerable to sector-specific shocks. A more balanced economy can provide better resilience against economic downturns.
4. Productivity and innovation: Strategic investment in areas like technology can drive productivity improvements and stimulate innovation, supporting long-term economic growth.

Whilst financial management remains crucial, it should not be prioritized at the expense of other important areas. A more balanced approach that considers both the short-term and long-term and values broad societal well-being alongside financial indicators, can support sustainable and inclusive economic growth.

Comparison with Other Developed Nations

In understanding the consequences of the UK's emphasis on financial management, it's beneficial to contrast it with the economic strategies of other developed nations. Countries such as Germany, Sweden, and the United States have different approaches to managing their economies, which offer valuable lessons and potential alternatives to the UK's current model. These nations have been successful in balancing financial management with technological advancement and societal welfare, providing rich case studies for the exploration of alternative economic models. In the sections below, we'll delve into each country's unique approach and assess the outcomes of their economic strategies.

Germany: Industrie 4.0

Germany's "Industrie 4.0" is a strategic initiative launched by the government to drive digital transformation in the manufacturing sector, which represents a significant portion of the country's economy. The initiative, which encourages businesses to adopt smart technologies and automation, has led to increased productivity and international competitiveness in German manufacturing. For example, Siemens, a German industrial manufacturing company, has significantly improved efficiency in their Amberg plant with advanced digital technologies, reducing defects by over 75% and improving productivity by around 1,400 products per employee annually (Kagermann, Wahlster & Helbig, 2013).

Sweden: Digital Transformation

Sweden has made significant strides in digital transformation, aided by strong government support and investment. A key focus area has been digitalization of public services, from healthcare to education. This strategy has led to increased accessibility and efficiency of these services. For instance, Stockholm's implementation of smart traffic management systems has helped decrease traffic congestion by 20% and emissions by 10%, contributing to a better quality of life (Stockholm City, 2018).

United States: Innovation Ecosystems

In contrast to the UK's austerity-focused approach, the United States emphasizes fostering innovation ecosystems through private enterprise and venture capital investment, often augmented by public research and development (R&D) funding. Silicon Valley, for example, is renowned for producing tech giants like Google and Facebook, driven by a combination of robust venture capital funding, supportive governmental policies, and strong connections with research institutions like Stanford University. This innovation-focused approach has helped the US to maintain its position as a global tech leader (Kenney & Patton, 2005).

The Need for Change and Its Implementation

The current focus on cost-minimization in technology investment is proving to be a disadvantage for UK companies in an increasingly digital global economy. In an era where technology underpins nearly every facet of business operation and growth, a failure to invest strategically in technology can lead to stagnation, decreased productivity, and a loss of competitiveness.

Why Change is Needed

With the rise of Industry 4.0, characterized by the merging of physical and digital technologies, the imperative to invest in technology has never been more urgent (Schwab, 2016). Furthermore, the COVID-19 pandemic has underscored the importance of digital readiness in ensuring business continuity amidst unprecedented disruptions (Bartik et al., 2020).

What Change Might Look Like:

6. The Hidden Cost of Saving

Change should involve a shift in perspective – from viewing technology investment as a cost to be minimized, to seeing it as a strategic tool for enhancing productivity, fostering innovation, and driving growth. This might involve:

1. Strategic Planning: The development of a long-term technology strategy aligned with the organization's overall objectives and priorities.
2. Investing in Infrastructure and Skills: Not just hardware and software, but also in human capital, ensuring employees have the necessary skills to adapt to new technologies.
3. Partnerships and Collaborations: Partnering with technology providers, startups, universities, or research institutions can help organizations stay abreast of the latest technological advancements.

Timeframe for Change

The timeframe for implementing these changes can vary significantly depending on the size of the organization, the industry in which it operates, and the specific technological investments required. That being said, change is typically a long-term process, often taking several years to fully implement and realize the benefits.

Starting the Change Process:

Starting the change process involves:

1. Leadership Commitment: Change must be championed at the highest level of the organization. Leadership must communicate the importance of technology investment and the need for change.
2. Assess Current Technology Capabilities: An audit of the current technology capabilities can help identify areas of strength and weakness.
3. Develop a Technology Strategy: Based on the audit, develop a technology strategy outlining the organization's technology goals, the investments required to achieve those goals, and a timeline for implementation.
4. Implementation and Review: Once the strategy is in place, the implementation process can begin. It's important to regularly review and adjust the strategy as needed based on the organization's evolving

needs and the rapidly changing technological landscape.

Ultimately, transitioning to a more strategic approach to technology investment is necessary for UK businesses to remain competitive. It's a long-term commitment that requires strategic planning, significant investment, and a shift in perspective. However, the potential rewards – increased productivity, improved staff satisfaction, and enhanced growth – make it a worthwhile endeavour.

Final Thoughts

This paper has (hopefully) shed light on the UK's prevailing cost-minimization approach to technology investment and its associated consequences. It has highlighted how this financially driven mindset has led to underinvestment in technology, leading to lower productivity, decreased staff satisfaction, and inhibited growth.

Comparison with other developed nations underscores the competitive disadvantage this approach confers, underscoring the need for a strategic shift. Through examples such as Google's growth propelled by its technology investments, and Kodak's downfall due to its failure to adapt digitally, we have seen the significant implications of technology investment decisions on a company's growth trajectory.

The necessity for change in the UK's technology investment strategy is clear. A transition from viewing technology as a cost to be minimized to recognizing it as a strategic tool for enhancing productivity, fostering innovation, and driving growth is needed.

Such change involves a commitment from leadership, strategic planning, investment in infrastructure and skills, and forming valuable partnerships. Although the timeframe for implementing these changes can be long, the potential rewards in terms of increased productivity, improved staff satisfaction, and enhanced growth make it a worthwhile endeavour.

As we navigate an increasingly digital global economy, strategic technology investment is not an optional extra, but an essential element of business strategy. For the UK to remain competitive, it is imperative to shift the focus from cost-minimization to strategic technology investment that aligns with long-term growth objectives.

In the final analysis, the cost of underinvestment in technology far outweighs the short-term savings. The long-term strategic benefits of technology investment make it a priority that UK businesses and policymakers cannot afford to overlook.

References

Bergh, A. (2011). The rise, fall and revival of a capitalist welfare state: what are the policy lessons from Sweden?. Research Institute of Industrial Economics (IFN), Stockholm.

Brynjolfsson, E., & Hitt, L. M. (2003). Computing productivity: Firm-level evidence. The Review of Economics and Statistics, 85(4), 793-808.

Brynjolfsson, E., & Hitt, L. M. (2000). Beyond computation: Information technology, organizational transformation and business performance. Journal of Economic perspectives, 14 (4), 23-48.

Harvey, D. (2005). A Brief History of Neoliberalism. Oxford University Press.

Kagermann, H., Wahlster, W., & Helbig, J. (2013). Recommendations for implementing the strategic initiative INDUSTRIE 4.0: Securing the future of German manufacturing industry; final report of the Industrie 4.0 Working Group. Forschungsunion.

Kenney, M., & Patton, D. (2005). Entrepreneurial geographies: Support networks in three high-tech industries. Economic Geography, 81(2), 201-228.

McKinsey Global Institute. (2017). Reinventing construction: A route to higher productivity. https://www.mckinsey.com/business-functions/operations/ourinsights/reinventing-construction-through-a-productivity-revolution

Mithas, S., Ramasubbu, N., & Sambamurthy, V. (2011). How information management capability influences firm performance. MIS Quarterly, 35(1), 237-256.

OECD. (2016). ICT investment as a share of value added. https://stats.oecd.org/Index.aspx?DataSetCode=ICT_INV

https://www.ons.gov.uk/economy/economicoutputandproductivity/productivitymeasur es/bulletins/internationalcomparisonsofproductivityfinalestimates/2016

Office for National Statistics. (2018). Labour productivity, UK: April to June 2018. https://www.ons.gov.uk/employmentandlabourmarket/peopleinwork/labourproductivit y/bulletins/labourproductivity/apriltojune2018

Office for National Statistics. (2018). International comparisons of UK productivity (ICP), final estimates: 2016.

Polder, M., Van Leeuwen, G., Mohnen, P., & Raymond, W. (2010). Product, process and organizational innovation: drivers, complementarity, and productivity effects. UNUMERIT, Maastricht Economic and Social Research and Training Centre on Innovation and Technology.

Statista. (2021). Google: Research & development expenditure 2004-2020.

Streeck, W. (1997). German capitalism: Does it exist? Can it survive?. New political economy, 2 (2), 237-256.

Stockholm City. (2018). Digitalization strategy for the city of Stockholm. https://start.stockholm/globalassets/start/om-oss/dokument/digitaliseringsstrategi-forstockholms-stad-2018-2021.pdf

https://www.statista.com/statistics/269606/expenditure-for-research-anddevelopment-of-google/

The Economist. (2012). The last Kodak moment? https://www.economist.com/business/2012/01/14/the-last-kodak-moment

Krysten M. Bacan & Rachael Evans MA, FCMI

7. Redefining Data Security: A Holistic Approach for Modern Organisations

Data Security, More than just Bits & Bytes. Data has become one of the most valuable assets a company has. It's an asset that comes with obligations and expectations as to how it is managed. And yet the conversation around organisational data security is often dominated by technological concerns. While discussions about IT systems, hacking, passwords, and malware are undoubtedly crucial, they represent only a fraction of the whole picture. In fact, a truly comprehensive approach to data security extends far beyond the domain of information technology, encompassing a multitude of other factors that are just as critical, yet often overlooked.

From the physical security of workspaces and the implementation of clear desk policies to nuanced considerations around third-party access and social engineering, a myriad of elements coalesce to form a holistic security framework. Add to this the complexity of insider trading, market abuse, and public messaging through marketing and communications, and it becomes evident that data security is a complex, multi-dimensional puzzle.

This article aims to provide a deep dive into these often-underemphasised aspects of organisational data security. We will examine how each factor, from physical access to role-based permissions and from user training to public communications, plays a pivotal role in fortifying an organisation's data security infrastructure. By understanding and addressing these variables, organisations can build a resilient and robust data security posture that is capable of withstanding not just the conventional technological threats, but also the more insidious and less-obvious vulnerabilities that put valuable data at risk.

Physical Access to Workspaces

While technological safeguards capture the limelight in discussions around organisational data security, physical access to workspaces is often underestimated. However, this facet of security is not to be trifled with; physical vulnerabilities can serve as entry points for a variety of data breaches.

Traditional mechanisms like entry badges, guest sign-ins, and surveillance cameras have not lost their relevance. These tools serve as the first line of defence against unauthorised entry. Multi-level authentication badges can prevent individuals from accessing departments or areas that handle sensitive information, while surveillance cameras can act as both a deterrent and a tool for post-incident analysis.

A front desk with security personnel is not the terminus of physical security; rather, it should be the beginning. Security measures need to be layered throughout the organisation. This could mean biometric access controls at data centres, alarmed doors for executive offices that contain sensitive information, or even simple methods known as 'mantraps' that consist of two interlocking doors that form a small, secured space between them. The doors are configured in such a way that both cannot be opened simultaneously.

A significant source of physical security risks is often visitors or temporary workers who are not fully acquainted with an organisation's security protocols. Utilising advanced Visitor Management Systems (VMS) can significantly mitigate these risks. These systems can screen, log, and monitor visitor movements, providing an additional security layer.

Physical security is not just about keeping external threats out but also managing internal threats. Tailgating—where an employee holds the door for someone without checking their credentials—can be an innocent action with severe consequences. Awareness campaigns can educate employees about the risks associated with such behaviour.

The layout and design of the workspace can also contribute to its security. A well-thought-out design can restrict the line of sight to sensitive areas or documents, discourage loitering, and guide visitor traffic to controlled areas, making illicit activities more easily detectable.

The effectiveness of physical security measures can wane over time due to complacency or wear and tear. Therefore, regular audits are crucial. These assessments should scrutinise the condition and functionality of locks, access controls, surveillance systems, and other security installations. Furthermore, they should evaluate the awareness and compliance levels among employees.

Clear Desk Policies

Amidst the frenzy of daily operations and looming deadlines, it is easy to underestimate the gravity of a cluttered workspace. Yet, a cluttered desk is more than an organisational faux pas—it represents a glaring security risk.

Even with a focus on digital data, paper documents still play a pivotal role in today's organisations. Draft contracts, employee data, meeting notes, or other sensitive information could be sitting out, visible to anyone who walks by. An unguarded desk could expose these documents to a variety of risks, from accidental leaks to malicious intent.

A Clear Desk Policy should be comprehensive and should outline the standard procedures for handling documents, including their storage, retrieval, and disposal. For instance, sensitive documents should be stored in locked filing cabinets, and confidential print jobs should not be left unattended. Employee training should accompany the policy rollout to ensure everyone understands both the 'what' and the 'why' behind these guidelines.

While a Clear Desk Policy focuses on physical copies of data, it is often beneficial to accompany this with measures aimed at securing digital data. When a computer is left unattended, even if only briefly, it becomes a security risk. Employing auto-lock mechanisms or screen savers requiring password authentication can serve as additional layers of protection.

A Clear Desk Policy should not be a mere suggestion but rather an organisational mandate. Regular checks or audits can ensure compliance. Employees should be educated about the policy and held accountable for compliance.

Beyond the tangible benefits of enhanced security, a Clear Desk Policy can also cultivate a more focused and disciplined work environment. When employees internalise the importance of keeping their workspace clean, it often translates into greater awareness and conscientiousness in other areas, including data management and security.

Third-party Access

In the intricate web of modern business relationships, third-party access to organisational data is often a necessary evil. From vendors to consultants and subcontractors, a plethora of external entities may require limited access to an organisation's internal data systems. While this collaborative approach fuels operational efficiency, it also opens up avenues for potential security risks.

One of the primary mechanisms to mitigate the risks associated with third-party access is Vendor Risk Management (VRM). This involves conducting comprehensive risk assessments before entering into any contracts. Such assessments examine the third-party's own data security protocols, ensuring they meet or exceed your organisation's standards.

When third-party entities are granted access, it should be under the principle of least privilege. This means providing only the minimal levels of access — or permissions — needed to perform the required tasks. Doing so limits the potential damage even if there's a breach in the third-party's own security systems.

All third-party access should be time-bound, meaning it should expire after a specific period or project completion. Additionally, real-time monitoring should be implemented to track what data is being accessed and for what purpose. Such logs can be crucial for audits and for investigating any anomalies or suspicious activities.

Legal agreements with third parties should explicitly detail the data to which they have access, the extent and limitations of this access, and the security protocols they must adhere to. Breach penalties and remediation processes should also be clearly outlined in the contract.

Third-party relationships should not be a 'set it and forget it' scenario. Regular audits can help ensure compliance with data security protocols, while periodic reviews can assess the continued necessity and appropriateness of the access granted.

Finally, it's important that internal staff understand the potential risks and protocols associated with third-party access. They should be trained to spot unusual activities that may signify a security breach and understand the procedures for granting, reviewing, and revoking third-party access rights.

Social Engineering

While technological vulnerabilities often capture the spotlight, human psychology can be exploited as a weak link in the security chain. Social engineering is the practice of manipulating individuals into divulging confidential information or performing actions that compromise security. It represents a psychological 'hack,' infiltrating an organisation by taking advantage of human behaviour and social interactions.

Various tactics fall under the umbrella of social engineering:

- **Phishing**: Deceptive emails that appear to come from a trusted source prompt the recipient to disclose personal information.
- **Pretexting**: The attacker fabricates a scenario (or pretext) to obtain information or access from the victim.
- **Tailgating**: Gaining physical entry into a restricted area by following an authorised person.
- **Baiting**: Leaving malware-infected physical devices in a location where the target will find them, hoping that curiosity will lead the target to insert the device into a computer.

The most effective antidote to social engineering is a well-informed staff. Regular training sessions should educate employees on recognising the signs of social engineering attempts and how to respond. Interactive training modules, simulated phishing campaigns, and real-world examples can make these sessions engaging and impactful.

Modern security systems can incorporate behavioural analytics to identify unusual actions that might signify a social engineering attack. For example, if an employee who has never accessed financial records suddenly attempts to do so, the action can be flagged for review. Creating specific policies that dictate how sensitive information is to be handled, shared, and confirmed can act as a guideline for employees. Strict "no tailgating" policies, multi-factor authentication, and procedures for verifying identity before releasing sensitive information can add layers of protection against social engineering tactics.

Creating an easily accessible reporting mechanism allows employees to promptly report any suspected social engineering attempt. Swift reporting can help contain the impact and prevent further damage.

User Training

Often, the most advanced security systems can be compromised by the simplest of errors, such as weak passwords or accidental sharing of confidential information. Such vulnerabilities underscore the critical role of user training in bolstering organisational data security.

User training should be comprehensive, covering a broad spectrum of topics, from basic password hygiene and two-factor authentication to the subtleties of recognising phishing attempts and social engineering tactics. The goal is to instil a culture of security mindfulness that permeates every aspect of an employee's work life.

Given the diverse range of roles within an organisation, a one-size-fits-all training program is unlikely to be effective. Modular training that is customised according to job roles can be more impactful. For example, the training for a finance department employee might emphasise the protocols around handling sensitive financial data, while training for front-desk personnel may focus on physical security and visitor management.

Effective training is not just theoretical but involves real-world simulations that mimic the types of challenges employees may face. Interactive phishing simulations, for instance, can provide practical experience in identifying deceptive emails. Mock scenarios can also be created to test the physical security awareness of employees, like the proper procedures when confronted with an unidentified individual attempting to access a restricted area.

Cyber threats evolve continually, and so should training programs. Regular updates and refresher courses can ensure that employees are abreast of the latest threats and countermeasures. This can also serve to reinforce earlier training and rectify any lapses in protocol adherence.

The effectiveness of user training programs should be periodically assessed through metrics such as test scores, incident reports, and direct feedback. This data can be invaluable in identifying areas for improvement and adapting the training to meet evolving needs.

Role-based Access

As organisations grow in complexity and scale, controlling who has access to what becomes increasingly intricate but ever more crucial. Role-based Access

Control (RBAC) offers a sophisticated yet pragmatic solution to this challenge by aligning data access permissions with job functions.

In RBAC, roles are defined based on the responsibilities and qualifications of a job description, and not the individual who fills the position. For instance, a "Financial Analyst" role would have access to certain financial databases but not to human resources records. When an employee occupies a role, they inherit these predefined permissions, minimising the potential for accidental or intentional misuse of data.

RBAC allows for granularity in access control. In a healthcare setting, for instance, a general practitioner may have access to basic patient histories but not to specialised psychiatric evaluations. This granularity extends beyond vertical hierarchies, allowing for a nuanced network of horizontal access controls that can reflect the complexities of modern organisations.

A well-implemented RBAC system makes it easier to comply with data protection regulations like GDPR or HIPAA. When access is systematically regulated and logged, auditing becomes a more straightforward process. This not only aids in regulatory compliance but also simplifies internal reviews to identify potential vulnerabilities.

RBAC systems can be dynamic, allowing permissions to be updated centrally. If a role's functions change or if new data resources are added, permissions can be updated in one location, rather than needing to update multiple user accounts. This scalability is particularly useful for larger organisations or those experiencing rapid growth.

While setting up an RBAC system might be technically straightforward, its success hinges on the understanding and cooperation of the staff who will use it. Training programs should include an overview of the RBAC system, its benefits, and its operating procedures. This becomes crucial during transitional phases, such as onboarding new employees or migrating to new software platforms.

Marketing and Communications

In an era where consumer engagement and brand visibility are indispensable for business success, organisations are increasingly turning to robust marketing and communication strategies. However, while these strategies bolster public image and customer relationships, they can inadvertently expose the organisation to security risks if not meticulously managed.

The narrative that an organisation disseminates publicly can sometimes reveal more than intended. For instance, a seemingly innocuous marketing campaign may hint at a new product feature, giving competitors or malicious actors clues to confidential projects. Therefore, marketing and communications teams must work closely with the organisation's data security experts to review all public messaging for unintentional disclosures.

Marketing campaigns often use a range of digital platforms, from social media to email newsletters. Each of these platforms is a potential entry point for cyber-attacks if not properly secured. This could range from the hacking of social media accounts to the exploitation of vulnerabilities in email marketing software.

Marketing often involves collecting customer data for analytics. The way this data is collected, stored, and utilised must be scrupulously compliant with data protection regulations. Failure to do so not only risks data breaches but can also result in substantial legal penalties.

Whether it's sales representatives detailing product features or customer service addressing client queries, staff interacting with customers must be trained in maintaining discretion about internal matters. Loose talk or inadvertent disclosure of sensitive information can have far-reaching consequences.

In the unfortunate event of a security breach, how the organisation communicates the incident to its stakeholders can impact its reputation and legal standing. A predefined crisis communication plan that addresses different scenarios must be in place. This plan should outline who will speak for the organisation, what will be disclosed, and the channels through which the communication will occur.

Insider Trading and Market Abuse

When one thinks of organisational data security, financial markets are not often the first consideration. However, insider trading and market abuse are significant concerns that hinge on the unauthorised use of privileged information. These activities not only have severe legal repercussions but also compromise the ethical foundations of an organisation.

Insider trading involves trading shares based on non-public, material information about the company. Market abuse could be a broader set of manipulations that include false reporting, spreading of rumours, or other deceptive practices intended to manipulate market prices. Both acts hinge on the misuse of confidential information that gives an unfair advantage to certain individuals.

Effective internal access controls are crucial to prevent insider trading and market abuse. Just as health records are restricted to certain roles in a healthcare setting, access to market-sensitive information should be stringently limited within financial departments or executive leadership.

Advanced surveillance technologies can monitor unusual trading activities within the organisation. Unexplained trades or sudden shifts in investment strategy can serve as red flags, prompting an internal review. Similarly, technology can monitor communications for trigger phrases or conversations that may indicate illicit activities.

Organisations must adhere to a litany of financial regulations designed to combat insider trading and market abuse, such as the Securities Exchange Act in the United States or the Market Abuse Regulation in the European Union. Compliance departments should ensure that all trading activities align with these legislative frameworks.

Regular training sessions should educate employees about the legal implications of insider trading and market abuse. Employees should also be aware of the internal reporting mechanisms for suspected abuse, which often include anonymous whistle-blower policies to protect those who report from reprisals.

The consequences of insider trading and market abuse extend beyond legal penalties. The reputational damage can be long-lasting and severe, affecting customer trust and stakeholder relations. Hence, an organisation's commitment to combating these issues reflects its broader ethical posture.

Conclusion: The Imperative of a Holistic and Sustained Approach to Data Security

As this comprehensive article has detailed, organisational data security is not merely a function of advanced technological measures designed to fend off external cyber threats. While the technological backbone—comprising firewalls, encryption algorithms, and malware detection systems—is indisputably crucial, it is but one chapter in the larger narrative of data security.

The physical dimensions of security, ranging from workspace access controls to clear desk policies, serve as a stark reminder that threats are not only virtual but also tangibly real. A lapse in physical security can swiftly negate the most stringent of digital safeguards, affirming the need for a balanced approach that respects both the virtual and the physical.

Similarly, human behaviour serves as a central fulcrum upon which security either thrives or falters. Social engineering, user training, and role-based access controls form critical sub-components that address this human element. Each employee, regardless of role, serves as a potential gateway for security breaches, underlining the imperative for comprehensive training and strict behavioural protocols.

The realm of marketing and communications, often seen as peripheral to data security concerns, comes into its own as a domain that requires vigilant governance. Likewise, the financial consequences of insider trading and market abuse add yet another layer of complexity, pointing to the intersectionality of organisational ethics, legal compliance, and data security.

In this complex and ever-changing landscape, static security measures are insufficient. The environment demands an adaptive strategy, one that evolves in response to emerging threats and incorporates advancements in security protocols. This need for adaptability further emphasises the requirement for ongoing training, regular audits, and periodic reassessment of security policies.

Moreover, the integrated approach to data security must be organisation-wide, cutting across departments and hierarchies. It calls for a collaborative effort that combines the expertise of IT professionals, human resources, legal advisors, and executive leadership. No department operates in a vacuum, and the success of any data security strategy relies on the symbiotic relationship between these diverse organisational units.

In sum, in an era where data is often termed 'the new oil,' safeguarding this invaluable resource requires a multi-faceted, continually evolving strategy. It's not just about erecting walls but also about educating those within them, not just about locking doors but also about scrutinising who holds the keys. The challenge is monumental but so too are the stakes. Fostering a culture of security awareness and implementing a holistic, sustained approach to data security is not merely advisable in this context—it is, without question, an existential necessity for modern organisations.

Rachael Evans MA, FCMI & Krysten M. Bacan

8. The Differentiation between Change Management and Project Management: An Analytical Perspective

In an era that has been characterised by unprecedented organisational complexities and continual change, the relevance of effective management strategies has attained new heights and deserves further conversations. This paper conducts an exhaustive examination of two distinct yet often conflated management paradigms: Change Management and Project Management. Grounded in a comprehensive review of academic literature, the paper aims to demystify these disciplines by first providing rigorous definitions and conceptual frameworks. It then embarks on a comparative analysis to elucidate their key similarities and differences, incorporating empirical data and case studies to offer a multi-dimensional perspective. The paper further investigates the critical factors that dictate the selection of one approach over the other, spotlighting the repercussions of incorrect choices on financial, strategic, and stakeholder dimensions. Lastly, it presents an in-depth profile comparison between Change Managers and Project Managers, emphasising their unique skills and roles. Interwoven with scholarly citations, this paper serves as an invaluable guide for organisational decision-makers, blending theoretical depth with practical insights.

Introduction

In today's Volatile, Uncertain, Complex, and Ambiguous (VUCA) world, the demand for effective management strategies has never been more acute. Organisations are increasingly grappling with rapid market shifts, technological disruptions, regulatory changes, and diverse stakeholder expectations. This ever-evolving landscape amplifies the relevance of two distinct yet frequently conflated managerial paradigms: Change Management and Project Management. The need to dissect, understand, and appropriately apply these disciplines is critical, not only for operational efficiency but also for long-term strategic success.

Considering the foregoing complexities, this scholarly paper embarks on an ambitious yet critical mission to dissect and delineate these two forms of management. It aims to accomplish this through a multi-layered analytical framework. The first layer involves providing rigorous definitions and conceptual underpinnings for both Change Management and Project Management, drawing from a wide array of authoritative academic sources to ground the discussion in established theories and models.

The second layer focuses on a comparative analysis, articulating both the commonalities and the differences that these management forms exhibit. Here, the paper incorporates empirical data and case studies, extending beyond theoretical conjectures to offer pragmatic insights into their practical applications and limitations.

The third analytical layer deepens the discourse by investigating the circumstances under which one management approach is preferable over the other. This part will scrutinise the potential risks and benefits, aiming to furnish organisational leaders with actionable guidelines. Additionally, the paper will delve into the often-overlooked consequences of incorrect approach selection, exploring how such mistakes can affect not just the immediate project or change initiative but also have a cascading impact on organisational health and stakeholder relationships.

Concluding the analytical framework, the paper will provide an exhaustive profile comparison between the roles of Change Managers and Project Managers. This will encompass an array of factors including—but not limited to—educational prerequisites, essential skill sets, generally accepted professional certifications, and overarching roles and responsibilities.

Interspersed throughout this multifaceted investigation will be scholarly citations and references, enhancing both the academic credibility and empirical validity of the paper's arguments. This exhaustive approach aspires to serve as an invaluable resource for decision-makers, academics, and practitioners alike, offering a balanced blend of theoretical depth and practical utility.

8. Change vs Project Management

Defining Change Management and Project Management

Understanding the core tenets and principles of Change Management and Project Management is critical for distinguishing between the two and for their effective implementation within an organisation.

Change Management

Conceptual Framework

Change management is a discipline anchored in social science theories, often drawing from fields as diverse as psychology, sociology, business management, and even anthropology. The ADKAR model, developed by Prosci's Jeff Hiatt, is one such conceptual framework that underscores the stages of change at an individual level, starting from Awareness, to Desire, Knowledge, Ability, and finally, Reinforcement (Hiatt, 2006).

Historical Evolution

Change management has its roots in the early and mid-20th century, during the evolution of the human relations theory. The 1980s and 1990s saw a surge in its importance, as scholars like John Kotter began to emphasise the role of leadership in effective change (Kotter, 1996).

Core Tenets

1. **People-Centric**: Unlike many management disciplines, change management places significant emphasis on human capital. It operates under the assumption that successful change is largely dependent on employee buy-in.
2. **Cultural Sensitivity**: Change management recognises the impact of organisational culture and values on the effectiveness of change strategies (Schein, 2010).
3. **Communication and Training**: These are considered vital tools for preparing an organisation for change, serving as vehicles for alignment and resistance management (Armenakis & Harris, 2009).

Project Management

Conceptual Framework

Project Management is predominantly underpinned by the Project Management Body of Knowledge (PMBOK), developed by the Project

Management Institute (PMI). It outlines key methodologies like Waterfall, Agile, and Scrum, offering structured approaches to project execution (Project Management Institute, 2017).

Historical Evolution

Unlike change management, project management has been an indispensable part of human civilisation for millennia, traceable to monumental projects like the Great Wall of China and the Egyptian pyramids. However, it wasn't until the mid-20th century that methodologies like Gantt charts and the Critical Path Method were developed, laying the foundation for modern project management (Morris, 1994).

Core Tenets

1. **Task-Oriented**: The primary focus is on discrete tasks that contribute to the completion of the overarching project goals.

2. **Time, Cost, and Scope**: Often referred to as the Project Management Triangle, these are the three main constraints that project managers must navigate (Atkinson, 1999).

3. **Quality Assurance**: Through rigorous monitoring and control, project management ensures that deliverables meet predetermined quality standards (Kerzner, 2013).

Key Similarities

While distinct in their primary focus and methods, Change Management and Project Management share fundamental similarities that can often lead to their conflation. This section aims to delve into these shared characteristics in a detailed manner.

Goal-Oriented Nature

Both Change Management and Project Management are intrinsically goal oriented. They are driven by a need to achieve specific objectives within an organisation, be it a change in culture or the completion of a physical project. The SMART criteria—Specific, Measurable, Achievable, Relevant, and Time-bound—are often applied in both domains to ensure that the objectives are well-defined and attainable (Doran, 1981).

Structured Methodology

The application of structured methodologies is a second key similarity. For example, Change Management often employs the ADKAR model, which provides a step-by-step guide to executing change (Hiatt, 2006). Similarly, Project Management utilizes methodologies like Waterfall or Agile, which dictate the sequence and scope of activities (Sutherland, 2014). These methodologies serve as foundational frameworks, providing a rigorous approach to the planning and execution phases.

Involvement of Stakeholders

Robust stakeholder engagement is another shared characteristic. Both Change Management and Project Management require a strong buy-in from internal and external stakeholders for successful implementation. This engagement involves communication, feedback loops, and often stakeholder-specific strategies to ensure alignment with organisational objectives (Freeman, 2010).

Resource Allocation and Management

Both fields emphasise the prudent allocation and management of resources—be it human, financial, or technological. Whether it's training programs in Change Management or budgeting in Project Management, effective resource management is essential for the success of both disciplines (Project Management Institute, 2017; Hiatt, 2006).

Risk Assessment and Management

Risk management is a core function in both disciplines. In Change Management, this might involve assessing the potential risks of employee resistance or cultural friction (Kotter, 1996). In Project Management, risk assessment often takes a more quantitative approach, examining the potential budget overruns or delays that might affect project outcomes (Hillson, 2003).

Performance Metrics and KPIs

Lastly, both fields are deeply committed to accountability and employ various Key Performance Indicators (KPIs) to measure success. While the metrics differ—often qualitative in Change Management and quantitative in Project Management—there is a common emphasis on setting benchmarks and monitoring performance against those metrics (Kerzner, 2013; Cummings & Worley, 2014).

Key Differences

Though they share similarities, Change Management and Project Management diverge fundamentally in several respects. This section aims to thoroughly explore the key areas where they differ.

Focus and Scope

The primary focus and scope differ distinctly between the two. Change Management is primarily concerned with the people side of change, dealing with how employees, teams, and entire organisations adapt to a new status quo (Kotter, 1996). Project Management, by contrast, centres around the execution of specific projects, generally related to products, services, or outcomes (Project Management Institute, 2017).

Temporal Dimension

Change Management often requires an indefinite timeline because behavioural and cultural changes do not have finite endpoints (Armenakis & Harris, 2009). Project Management is inherently time-bound, with a specific start and end date (Atkinson, 1999).

Success Metrics

The metrics for success vary considerably. In Change Management, success might be gauged by levels of employee engagement, reduction in turnover, or a palpable shift in organisational culture (Schein, 2010). In Project Management, success is often quantified by on-time delivery, staying within budget, and meeting specified quality standards (Kerzner, 2013).

Leadership and Management Skills

The skill set required for leadership also differs. Change managers often require strong emotional intelligence, negotiation abilities, and a knack for cultural sensitivity (Cameron & Green, 2019). Project managers, on the other hand, need a robust understanding of planning, scheduling, risk management, and stakeholder management (Schwalbe, 2018).

Methodological Approaches

The methodologies employed are often different as well. Change Management uses models like ADKAR or Kotter's 8-Step Process, which are less structured compared to Project Management methodologies like Agile, Waterfall, or Scrum, which are often rigid and well-defined (Sutherland, 2014; Hiatt, 2006).

Resource Prioritization

Change Management typically prioritises human capital and focuses on soft skills like communication, training, and leadership (Cummings & Worley, 2014). In Project Management, the emphasis is more on hard skills and resources like budgeting, scheduling, and quality assurance (Project Management Institute, 2017).

When to Choose One Over the Other

The question of whether to adopt a Change Management or Project Management approach hinges on several critical factors. This section elucidates these factors in greater depth.

Nature of the Task

One of the most definitive indicators is the nature of the task at hand. If the primary objective involves changing behaviours, attitudes, or organisational culture, then Change Management is the logical choice (Burnes, 2004). If the goal is to deliver a specific product, service, or outcome within a fixed timeframe, Project Management is more apt (Project Management Institute, 2017).

Complexity and Scale

For complex and large-scale transformations involving multiple departments or organisations, a hybrid approach incorporating both Change Management and Project Management may be beneficial (Cameron & Green, 2019).

Urgency and Time Constraints

The timeline can also be decisive. Quick, high-impact projects may be better served by Project Management's structured and time-bound approach. However, if the change is to be sustained over the long term and deeply integrated into the organisational fabric, Change Management is preferable (Kotter, 1996).

Resource Availability

In scenarios where considerable resources—be it human, financial, or technological—are readily available, Project Management may be more suitable given its often resource-intensive nature (Schwalbe, 2018). For initiatives where human capital is the primary resource, Change Management becomes a more practical choice (Hiatt, 2006).

Stakeholder Impact

When the impact of the change primarily affects the employees or organisational culture, then Change Management is crucial to ensure the successful transition and acceptance of new behaviours or practices (Cummings & Worley, 2014). In contrast, when the impact is primarily on external stakeholders, such as clients or customers, Project Management could be more effective (Atkinson, 1999).

Risk Profile

The risk factors also influence the choice. If the risks primarily involve human capital or cultural resistance, a Change Management approach is more fitting (Armenakis & Harris, 2009). On the other hand, if the risks are more quantitative—like budget overruns or schedule delays—Project Management is the appropriate method (Hillson, 2003).

The Consequences Behind an Incorrect Approach Choice

Selecting an inappropriate methodology—be it Change Management or Project Management—can have far-reaching consequences that are not only costly but also potentially detrimental to organisational integrity.

Financial Implications

Opting for the wrong approach can result in significant financial ramifications. For example, adopting a Project Management approach to cultural change may lead to budget overruns due to underestimating the complexities involved in human behaviour change (Meredith & Mantel, 2011). Conversely, employing Change Management tactics for a time-sensitive project may result in financial losses due to delays (Piderit, 2000).

Employee Morale and Turnover

Mismatched approaches can contribute to low employee morale and increased turnover. Employees subjected to a poorly executed change strategy are more likely to leave the organisation, resulting in a loss of valuable human capital and added costs for recruitment and training (Herscovitch & Meyer, 2002).

Stakeholder Confidence

Using an incorrect approach may erode stakeholder confidence. For example, if a project that calls for rigid timelines and fixed deliverables is managed using a Change Management framework, stakeholders may lose faith in the organisation's ability to deliver (Atkinson, 1999).

Organisational Reputation

Organisational reputation can suffer. Whether it is failing to deliver on a project or an inability to implement successful change, the long-term damage to an organisation's credibility can have a domino effect, including the potential loss of market share or the failure to attract top talent (Fombrun, 1996).

Quality of Work

The quality of the project or change initiative can be significantly compromised. The methodologies and tools employed in Change Management and Project Management are tailored to their respective objectives; using them interchangeably can lead to sub-optimal results (Cameron & Green, 2019).

Strategic Misalignment

Finally, there can be a strategic misalignment within the organisation. Inaccurate approach selection can divert resources and focus from other critical areas, leading to incongruities in achieving the broader organisational objectives (Kaplan & Norton, 2008).

Profile Differences: Change Manager vs. Project Manager

Though both Change Managers and Project Managers are vital to the success of organisational initiatives, their roles, competencies, and methodologies markedly differ.

Educational Background

Change Managers often possess backgrounds in psychology, sociology, or human resources, equipping them to handle the complexities of human behaviour (Caldwell, 2003). Project Managers, on the other hand, frequently have backgrounds in business, engineering, or information technology, which provides them with the technical know-how for project execution (Schwalbe, 2018).

Skill Sets

Change Manager

- **Emotional Intelligence**: Adept at perceiving and navigating the emotional landscape of an organisation (Goleman, 1998).

- **Negotiation Skills**: Skilled in balancing various stakeholder interests for organisational change (Fisher & Ury, 1981).

- **Conflict Resolution**: Expertise in resolving interpersonal and departmental conflicts, often a by-product of change (Rahim, 2002).

Project Manager

- **Risk Management**: Proficient in identifying and mitigating risks associated with project delivery (Hillson, 2003).

- **Scheduling**: Expertise in creating and managing timelines to ensure on-time project delivery (Kerzner, 2013).

- **Budget Management**: Ability to manage financial resources effectively (Meredith & Mantel, 2011).

Professional Certifications

Change Managers often hold certifications like Prosci's Change Management Certification or ACMP's Certified Change Management Professional (CCMP) (Prosci, 2020; ACMP, 2020). Project Managers frequently have PMP (Project Management Professional) or PRINCE2 credentials (Project Management Institute, 2017; AXELOS, 2017).

Roles and Responsibilities

Change Managers focus on preparing, equipping, and supporting employees to successfully adopt change (Cameron & Green, 2019). Project Managers concentrate on project planning, execution, and closing, ensuring that projects meet the predefined objectives within the given constraints (Schwalbe, 2018).

Conclusion

Change Management and Project Management are distinctive approaches that offer unique value to organisations. Though they share similarities, such as the overarching aim to improve organisational performance, their focal points, methodologies, and outcomes are markedly different. The former is concerned primarily with people and behavioural modifications, while the latter focuses on the attainment of specific deliverables within predefined parameters.

The choice between these two approaches is often nuanced and based on several variables such as the nature of the task, complexity, urgency, resource availability, and stakeholder impact. The repercussions of selecting an inappropriate approach can be far-reaching, affecting the organisation's financial health, employee morale, stakeholder confidence, and overall strategic alignment.

Additionally, the professional profiles of Change Managers and Project Managers differ substantively, with each offering a unique set of skills and expertise tailored to specific organisational needs. Recognising these profile differences is paramount for the appropriate allocation of human resources in either change or project initiatives.

Therefore, it is incumbent upon organisational decision-makers to conduct a meticulous assessment of their specific needs, challenges, and objectives to determine the most suitable approach. This choice is not merely a procedural one; it is a strategic decision that can significantly influence the organisation's future trajectory.

References

ACMP. (2020). *CCMP Certification Handbook*. Association of Change Management Professionals.

Armenakis, A., & Harris, S. (2009). Reflections: our Journey in Organizational Change Research and Practice. *Journal of Change Management, 9(2), 127-142.*

Atkinson, R. (1999). Project Management: Cost, Time and Quality, Two Best Guesses and a Phenomenon, It's Time to Accept Other Success Criteria. *International Journal of Project Management, 17(6), 337-342.*

AXELOS. (2017). *Managing Successful Projects with PRINCE2*. TSO (The Stationery Office).

Bridges, W., & Mitchell, S. (2019). *Managing Transitions: Making the Most of Change*. Nicholas Brealey.

Burnes, B. (2004). *Managing Change: A Strategic Approach to Organizational Dynamics*. Pearson Education.

Caldwell, R. (2003). The Changing Roles of Personnel Managers: Old Ambiguities, New Uncertainties. Journal of Management Studies, 40(4), 983-1004.

Cameron, E., & Green, M. (2019). Making Sense of Change Management. Kogan Page.

Crawford, L. (2005). Senior management perceptions of project management competence. International Journal of Project Management, 23(1), 7-16.

Cummings, T.G., & Worley, C.G. (2014). Organization Development and Change. Cengage learning.

Doran, G. T. (1981). There's a S.M.A.R.T. way to write management's goals and objectives. Management Review, 70(11), 35-36.

Fisher, R., & Ury, W. (1981). Getting to Yes: Negotiating Agreement Without Giving In. Penguin Books.

Freeman, R.E. (2010). Strategic management: A stakeholder approach. Cambridge University Press.

Goleman, D. (1998). Working with Emotional Intelligence. Bantam Books.

Herscovitch, L., & Meyer, J.P. (2002). Commitment to Organizational Change: Extension of a Three-Component Model. Journal of Applied Psychology, 87(3), 474–487.

Hiatt, J. (2006). ADKAR: a model for change in business, government and our community. Prosci.

Hillson, D. (2003). Effective Opportunity Management for Projects: Exploiting Positive Risk. Marcel Dekker.

Kaplan, R.S., & Norton, D.P. (2008). The Execution Premium: Linking Strategy to Operations for Competitive Advantage. Harvard Business Press.

Kerzner, H. (2013). Project Management: A Systems Approach to Planning, Scheduling, and Controlling. John Wiley & Sons.

Kotter, J.P. (1996). Leading Change. Harvard Business Press.

Kerzner, H. (2013). Project Management: A Systems Approach to Planning, Scheduling, and Controlling. John Wiley & Sons.

Marks, M.L., & Mirvis, P.H. (2011). Merge Ahead: A Research Agenda to Increase Merger and Acquisition Success. Human Resource Management, 50(1), 151-176.

Meredith, J.R., & Mantel, S.J. (2011). Project Management: A Managerial Approach. John Wiley & Sons.

Morris, P.W.G. (1994). The Management of Projects. Thomas Telford.

Müller, R., & Turner, R. (2010). Leadership competency profiles of successful project managers. International Journal of Project Management, 28(5), 437-448.

Piderit, S.K. (2000). Rethinking Resistance and Recognizing Ambivalence: A Multidimensional View of Attitudes Toward an Organizational Change. Academy of Management Review, 25(4), 783-794.

Pinto, J.K. (2019). Project management: achieving competitive advantage. Pearson.

Project Management Institute. (2017). A Guide to the Project Management Body of Knowledge (PMBOK® Guide). PMI Publications.

Prosci. (2020). Prosci Change Management Certification Program Overview. Prosci Inc.

Pugh, L. (2016). Change Management in Information Services. Routledge.

Rahim, M.A. (2002). Toward a Theory of Managing Organizational Conflict. The International Journal of Conflict Management, 13(3), 206-235.

Schein, E.H. (2010). Organizational Culture and Leadership. John Wiley & Sons.

Schwalbe, K. (2018). Information Technology Project Management. Cengage Learning.

Sutherland, J. (2014). Scrum: The Art of Doing Twice the Work in Half the Time. Crown Business.

Turner, R. (2014). The Handbook of Project-Based Management. McGraw-Hill.

Section Two:
People

Rachael Evans MA, FCMI

9. Balancing Expertise and Leadership: The Value of Retaining Subject Matter Experts as Individual Contributors

The evolution of a successful organisation involves carefully balancing the roles of subject matter experts (SMEs) and management personnel. Traditionally, the career trajectory has led many SMEs into managerial roles, often at the expense of their individual contributions. However, the value of allowing SMEs to remain as individual contributors cannot be overstated.

So just what are the advantages and disadvantages of both approaches? Let's have a quick look using a few real-world examples.

The Traditional Path: SMEs as Managers

Advantages

1. **Enhanced Decision Making:** When an SME becomes a manager, they bring their specialised knowledge to decision-making processes. Marissa Mayer, a Stanford University graduate with a specialisation in Artificial Intelligence, was one of the first engineers at Google. Her understanding of the product deeply influenced her leadership and decision-making when she later became Yahoo's CEO.

2. **Mentoring and Training:** SMEs in leadership roles can also expedite the learning curve for junior team members. They are in a unique position to train and mentor others. In the world of film, director Steven Spielberg, who started as an expert in the art of storytelling, rose to management as a film director. His expertise has fostered the growth of many aspiring filmmakers

Disadvantages

1. **Management Overload:** SMEs promoted to managerial roles often face overwhelming administrative and people-management duties that take them away from their area of expertise. For example, Bill Gates, co-founder and former CEO of Microsoft, transitioned from a hands-on programming role to a more managerial position, which reduced his time spent on innovative software development.

2. **Skill Mismatch:** Not all SMEs are naturally skilled in leadership or have the desire to lead. When forced into these roles, the results can be detrimental. Renowned physicist and Nobel laureate Richard Feynman reportedly turned down an offer to become a dean at Caltech because he believed he could contribute more effectively in his individual role.

The New Perspective: SMEs as Individual Contributors

Advantages

1. Continual Innovation: When SMEs continue to work as individual contributors, they can focus more on their areas of expertise and continue to innovate. Tim Berners-Lee, for instance, the inventor of the World Wide Web, has remained a contributor to the evolution of Internet standards and technologies, providing significant ongoing value in his area of expertise.

9. Balancing Expertise and Leadership

2. Deep Domain Expertise: By remaining individual contributors, SMEs can continue to deepen their specialised knowledge. Linus Torvalds, the creator of Linux, for instance, has chosen to remain deeply involved in coding and development, ensuring that his mastery of the subject continues to benefit the open-source community.

Disadvantages

1. Limited Influence: SMEs who remain as individual contributors may have limited influence over strategic decisions and broader team direction.
2. Career Growth: Some organisations equate career progression with leadership roles, which may leave SMEs who prefer to remain as individual contributors with limited opportunities for career advancement.

The path an SME takes should depend on their personal aspirations, their organisation's needs, and the value they can deliver in either role. Retaining SMEs as individual contributors can bring significant value and innovation to an organisation. It's crucial for organisations to recognise this potential and create a supportive environment that nurtures and rewards expertise as much as leadership.

Krysten M. Bacan

10. Embracing Change: The Benefits of Hiring a Fractional CIO/CTO for Small to Medium-Sized Organizations

This article discusses the signs and indicators that a small to medium-sized organization should consider when determining whether to change its approach to information technology and hire a fractional or part-time technology manager. One strategy increasingly being adopted is the hiring of a fractional or part-time Chief Information Officer (CIO) or Chief Technology Officer (CTO) to oversee IT operations and strategy. This article outlines the signs and indicators that suggest an organization is ready for this change, the benefits of hiring a fractional leader, and the skills required for success.

Signs and Indicators that a Company is Ready for a Fractional CIO/CTO

- Rapid growth: As companies expand, the complexity of their IT systems and infrastructure increases, requiring expert management (1).
- Inability to keep up with industry advancements: Falling behind in the adoption of new technologies can lead to a loss of competitive advantage (2).
- Frequent downtime or security breaches: Inefficient or outdated IT systems can result in operational interruptions and costly data breaches (3).

- Lack of in-house IT expertise: Small to medium-sized organizations may back the resources for a full-time CIO/CTO (4).

Why a Fractional Leader?

- Cost-effectiveness: A part-time CIO/CTO allows companies to access high-level expertise without the expense of a full-time executive (5).
- Flexibility: Fractional leaders can be brought in as needed to address specific IT challenges or projects (6).
- Strategic guidance: Part-time CIOs/CTOs can help organizations develop and implement forward-thinking IT strategies (7).

Skills Required for a Fractional CIO/CTO

- Hard Skills: Technical expertise, cybersecurity, project management, and knowledge of industry-specific software and systems (8).
- Soft Skills: Strong communication, leadership, problem-solving, and strategic thinking abilities (9).

Consequences of Not Adapting

- Lost opportunities: Organizations that fail to invest in IT expertise may miss out on opportunities to streamline operations and increase profitability (12).
- Decreased competitiveness: Companies that neglect technological advancements risk falling behind their competitors (13).
- Reputational damage: Security breaches and IT failures can lead to negative publicity and loss of consumer trust (14).

Hiring a Fractional CIO/CTO: Key Considerations

- Hard Skills: Verify the candidate's technical expertise and industry knowledge through certifications, previous work experience, and references (15).
- Soft Skills: Assess the candidate's communication, leadership, and strategic thinking abilities through interviews and behavioural assessments (16).

10. Embracing Change

- Cultural fit: Ensure the candidate shares the organization's values and vision (17).

Conclusion

Small to medium-sized organizations must remain vigilant and adaptable in today's dynamic technological environment. Hiring a fractional CIO/CTO can provide a cost-effective and flexible solution for companies seeking to enhance their IT operations and maintain a competitive edge. By identifying the signs that indicate the need for change and understanding the benefits of a fractional leader, organiza2ons can make informed decisions about their IT strategies. When hiring a frac2onal CIO/CTO, it is crucial to evaluate both hard and soft skills, as well as ensuring a good cultural fit within the organization.

References

(1) DeloiFe. (2020). The Growth Dilemma: How Small and Medium Businesses Can Scale Up with IT. Retrieved from http://www2.deloiFe.com/content/dam/DeloiFe/global/Documents/Technology/gxscaling- up-it-for-smb.pdf

(2) McKinsey & Company. (2019). Digital Strategy in a Time of Crisis. Retrieved from http://www.mckinsey.com/business-func2ons/mckinsey-digital/our-insights/digitalstrategy-in-a-2me-of-crisis

(3) IBM. (2021). Cost of a Data Breach Report. Retrieved from http://www.ibm.com/security/data-breach

(4) Gartner. (2020). Building a Scalable IT Team for Small and Medium-Sized Businesses. Retrieved from http://www.gartner.com/en/documents/3983122/building-a-scalable-itteam-for-small-and-medium-sized

(5) CIO Magazine. (2018). The Rise of the Frac2onal CIO. Retrieved from http://www.cio.com/ar2cle/3297749/the-rise-of-the-frac2onal-cio.html

(6) Forbes Technology Council. (2019). 12 Signs You Should Invest in a Frac2onal CTO. Retrieved from http://www.forbes.com/sites/forbestechcouncil/2019/09/05/12-signs-youshould-invest-in-a-frac2onal-cto/?sh=38f7d647344d

(7) TechRepublic. (2019). How a Part-Time CIO Can Help SMBs with Digital Transforma2on. Retrieved from http://www.techrepublic.com/ar2cle/how-a-part-2me-cio-can-help-smbswith-digital-transforma2on/

(8) HBR. (2018). The Hard and So@ Skills of a Successful CIO. Retrieved from http://hbr.org/2018/09/the-hard-and-so@-skills-of-a-successful-cio

(9) IDC. (2020). The Changing Role of the CIO in the Digital Era. Retrieved from http://www.idc.com/getdoc.jsp?containerId=US44829718

(10) Acme Corp Case Study. (2022). The Impact of a Frac2onal CIO on Opera2onal Efficiency. Retrieved from http://www.acmecorp.com/case-studies/frac2onal-cio

(11) Beta Inc Case Study. (2022). Naviga2ng Digital Transforma2on with a Part-Time CTO. Retrieved from http://www.betainc.com/case-studies/part-2me-cto

(12) PwC. (2019). The Cost of Doing Nothing: Why Failing to Invest in IT Can Hurt Your Business. Retrieved from http://www.pwc.com/us/en/services/consul2ng/technology/costof-doing-nothing.html

(13) Accenture. (2020). Bridging the Digital Divide for Small and Medium Enterprises. Retrieved from http://www.accenture.com/_acnmedia/PDF-121/Accenture-Bridging-Digital-Divide-SME.pdf (14) Cisco. (2019). Small Business Reputa2on and the Cost of Cybersecurity. Retrieved from http://www.cisco.com/c/dam/en_us/about/security-center/assets/small-businessmaterials/cisco-sbr-infographic.pdf

(15) IT World. (2018). How to Assess the Hard Skills of a CIO/CTO Candidate. Retrieved from http://www.itworld.com/ar2cle/3273362/how-to-assess-the-hard-skills-of-a-cio-ctocandidate.html

(16) CIO Magazine. (2020). 7 So@ Skills Every CIO Needs to Thrive. Retrieved from http://www.cio.com/ar2cle/3445440/7-so@-skills-every-cio-needs-to-thrive.html

(17) The Enterprisers Project. (2019). IT Culture Change: How to Hire for BeFer Fit. Retrieved from http://enterprisersproject.com/ar2cle/2019/2/it-culture-change-hire-fit

Suggested Additional Readings

NACD. (2019). Aligning IT and Business Strategy: A Board's Role in Oversight. Retrieved from https://www.nacdonline.org/en/insights/publications.cfm?ItemNumber=65565

MIT Sloan Management Review. (2018). Bridging the Leadership Gap between Tech and

Business. Retrieved from https://sloanreview.mit.edu/article/bridging-the-leadership-gapbetween- tech-and-business/

Gartner. (2021). The Future of IT Leadership: Five New Capabilities CIOs Need to Succeed. Retrieved from https://www.gartner.com/en/conferences/emea/cio-uk

By staying informed about the latest trends and best practices, small to medium-sized organizations can strategically position themselves to adapt to the rapidly changing technological landscape. Embracing a fractional CIO/CTO model can empower these organizations to streamline operations, increase profitability, and maintain a competitive edge in their respective industries. As organizations continue to navigate the digital era, it is essential to prioritize the hiring and development of skilled technology leaders who can guide businesses towards a successful future.

Rachael Evans MA, FCMI

11. Contractor to Consultant, can one become the other?

I'm currently in a contract and I wish to become a consultant. How do I go about this?

This is a very common question so I've opted to offer some insight into the differences, constraints, and how, if appropriate, one might go about making the change. I'll start by offering that both contractors and consultants play unique and invaluable roles. Both bring a wealth of expertise, but their approaches and interactions with clients can differ in meaningful ways.

From daily operations to financial agreements, and even the legal ties that bind, the two roles navigate distinct terrains. For those looking to transition from hands-on contractors to strategic consultants, it's a journey of growth, discovery, and deepened relationships. I hope to offer you a guide through these nuances, highlighting the importance of understanding, adaptability, and clear communication in fostering fruitful collaborations.

Introduction

Within professional services, understanding the nuances between different engagement models is crucial. Two of the most juxtaposed roles in this sphere are contractors and consultants. While both offer specialised services to businesses or individuals, the nature of their engagement, deliverables, and value propositions can vary considerably.

At first glance, the distinction may appear to be semantic, perhaps even trivial. However, the implications of these roles stretch across operational models, financial structures, legal considerations, and the very essence of service delivery. A comprehensive appreciation of these differences is essential not only for organisations seeking the right expertise but also for professionals navigating their career trajectories or considering transitions between these roles.

Role Definitions

When evaluating the options surrounding the engagement of external expertise, one of the first considerations businesses must confront is defining the nature of the engagement they seek. Is it the hands-on expertise of someone to execute a predefined task? Or is it the strategic acumen of a seasoned professional to navigate complex challenges? At the core of this decision lies the differentiation between contractors and consultants. Each term embodies a distinct paradigm of service delivery, shaped by their fundamental roles and the nature of their engagements.

As we examine their respective definitions and roles, it becomes evident that these distinctions influence not just the immediate scope of work but the broader interactions and relationships between the professional and the organisation.

So, just what are the primary differences between the roles?

Contractor

- **Depth:** Often hired to execute a specific task or series of tasks. For example, in the IT world, a contractor might be hired to develop a specific module of a software application. In construction, a contractor might be hired to lay the foundation of a building.
- **Duration:** The engagement is usually for the duration of a project or until a specific deliverable is complete. Once the task is finished, the contract ends unless extended or renewed.
- **Supervision:** Often works under the client's direction and might report to someone within the client's organisation.

Consultant

- **Depth:** Engaged to leverage their specialised knowledge or expertise to address complex problems or decisions. For example, a business consultant might be brought in to streamline operations or suggest growth strategies.
- **Duration:** The length of engagement varies but can often be shorter than contractors because they're offering strategic insights rather than hands-on execution.

11. Contractor to Consultant, can one become the other?

- **Supervision**: They function with greater autonomy and don't typically report to anyone within the client's organisation.

Operational Differences

The first section above sets the tone for the differences between the two roles, but we need to go deeper into how they differ. Beyond the contractual constraints, the day-to-day mechanics of how services are rendered open define the success and fluidity of an engagement. While the fundamental roles of contractors and consultants are distinct, these differences become even more pronounced when examining their operational modus operandi. From integrational into client teams to the tools and methodologies employed, the operational contours of these roles not only impact project outcomes but also influence organisational cultures and workflows.

Let's look deeper at what the differences look like from an operational perspective as an expansion of the above definitions.

Contractor

- **Integration:** Might have an email address with the client's domain, attend regular meetings, and be indistinguishable from an employee in daily operations.
- **Tools & Resources:** Often uses the client's systems, software, and resources to perform their tasks.
- **On-site Requirement**: Many contractors, especially in roles like IT or construction, might be required to work on-site.

Consultant

- **Integration**: Typically remains distinct from the client's internal teams, emphasising their outsider and expert perspective.
- **Tools & Resources**: Brings their own proprietary tools, models, or methodologies into their consulting practice.
- **On-site Requirement**: Their work might be conducted off-site, with periodic onsite meetings for briefings or presentations.

Financial Differences

Once we understand the key operational and engagement differences, we next need to explore how the variation in engagement models impacts the financial considerations. Here, after all, is where the question originates from. Namely, how much and how am I going to get paid for this engagement?

However, the financial architecture of a professional engagement doesn't merely underscore the monetary exchange between pares; it offers a lens into the perceived value, risk distribution, and commitment levels inherent in the collaboration. Contractors and consultants, despite their overlapping realms of expertise, open navigate distinct financial landscapes. These distinctions, rooted in their differing roles and operational modalities, manifest in billing structures, expense allocations, and even performance-based incentives.

Contractor

- **Billing**: Predominantly billed based on time – hourly or daily rates. In some cases, might be a fixed-price contract based on deliverables.
- **Expenses**: Depending on the contract, expenses might be borne by the client.

Consultant:

- **Billing**: Diverse structures, including hourly, retainer-based, or value-based pricing. Some consultants might even take a percentage of the savings or revenue they help generate.
- **Expenses**: Typically charge expenses back to the client, especially if specialised resources or travel is involved.

And of course, there are many local taxation issues such as the UK's IR35 constraints that will frame the financial approach. If, for example, you have a single client in the same location and the expectation is that you alone can fulfil the terms, then it might not be appropriate financially. However, if you've come looking for the answer to the taxation issue, I'm afraid that I can't help in this aspect, you need professional advice on this.

Legal and Contractual Differences

Clearly, if the operating model differs, there are financial variances, this will emanate in the contractual engagement model itself as the legal and contractual frameworks serve as the binding threads, ensuring clarity, safeguarding interests, and setting the stage for mutual accountability.

11. Contractor to Consultant, can one become the other?

The realms of contractors and consultants, though intertwined in the broader spectrum of external expertise, are governed by distinct legal considerations. These divergences not only capture the essence of their unique service offerings but also address the varied risks, intellectual property concerns, and responsibilities inherent in their roles.

Contractor

- **Liability**: Often carry insurance for their work, especially if they are in fields where errors can have significant financial consequences.
- **Scope**: The contract will have a detailed scope of work, often with milestones.

Consultant

- **Liability**: Might have clauses that limit their liability, especially since their work is advisory and execution rests with the client.
- **Scope**: While the scope of work is defined, it often leaves room for flexibility as the consultancy progresses and the needs and expectations evolve.

If you were engaged via an agency, look at the terms of engagement, they may very well limit what, when or how you engage with 'their' client. It may be that you need to be brave and accept that the move from contractor to consultant is a much bigger move than a change in title and that consulting engagements are complex, and require different contracts, insurance, compliance, and taxation considerations. All our consulting engagements require the use of initial NDAs, master agreements, and Statements of Work. We have insurance policies in place, we provide tools, systems, processes, financial and accounting background operational processes.

Transitioning your current engagement from a Contractor to a Consultant

Ok, so you're still here, you're keen to explore if its possible to convert your current engagement from one model to another. I respect that, so, let's continue onwards.

Transitioning from the role of a contractor to that of a consultant is more than just a change in title—it represents a shift in perspective, responsibility, and the value you bring to your clients. The key is to approach the conversation with clarity, confidence, and genuine intent to align your consultancy aspirations with your client's business objectives. This of course is underlined with a host of considerations.

1. **Shift in Mindset**: Move from a task-oriented mindset to a solution-oriented one. Understand the broader implications of your expertise.
2. **Branding**: Position yourself as an expert. This might involve writing articles, speaking at conferences, or publishing research.
3. **Negotiation Skills**: Learn to negotiate contracts that reflect the value of your expertise and not just time spent.
4. **Relationship Building**: Cultivate relationships with decision-makers who can benefit from your consultancy, not just those who need tasks executed.
5. **Ongoing Education**: Consultants need to be at the forefront of their fields, so continuous learning and certification are crucial.

Of course, bear in mind that the nature and manner of your initial engagement may of course mean that transitioning your current engagement may not be practical or appropriate. As a contractor do you use a third-party agency for example? You need to be willing to accept that your current engagement and relationship started and will remain as a contracting engagement.

Don't worry, I'm not going to end it there, I'll dive a little deeper for you as if you've spent the me to read this far, you deserve a little more. So, let's open the list a bit further and add a few steps that should help you both open and then drive the conversation.

Self-Assessment and Preparation:

- Knowledge: Ensure you're up to date with the latest trends, tools, and strategies in your field.
- Skillset Enhancement: Identify any gaps in your skills or knowledge and seek training or certifications as needed.
- Value Proposition: Clearly define what makes your consultancy offering unique and valuable.

11. Contractor to Consultant, can one become the other?

Initiating the Dialogue:

- Timing: Choose a moment when you've recently delivered value, such as after successful project completion.
- Setting: Opt for a one-on-one meeting where you can discuss your transition without interruptions.
- Transparency: Clearly convey the reasons for your transition, emphasising the added value it will bring to your client.

Presenting Your New Role:

- Demonstrate Value: Use past achievements as a contractor to illustrate how a consultancy model would amplify those successes.
- Show Flexibility: While you're introducing a new model, assure your client of your commitment to adapt to their evolving needs.
- Provide Testimonials: If you've already started consulting for other clients, share their feedback and success stories.

Navigating Concerns:

- Acknowledge and Address: Clients might have reservations about the new model. Listen actively and address their concerns with concrete examples and solutions.
- Reiterate Commitment: Emphasise your dedication to their business objectives, regardless of your professional title or engagement model.

Redefining Contractual Agreements:

- Clarity in Scope: Clearly outline the scope of your consultancy, setting boundaries while leaving room for flexibility.
- Billing and Terms: Transition from hourly or task-based billing to a model that might be retainer-based, project-based, or value-driven.
- Performance Metrics: Establish new metrics or KPIs that reflect the strategic nature of your consultancy.

Maintain Open Communication:

- Feedback Loops: Establish regular check-ins to ensure alignment and gather feedback on the evolving consultancy model.

- Continuous Evolution: As the relationship matures, be open to refining your consultancy model based on the unique needs of each client.

Embracing the Evolution

The nuanced differences between a contractor and a consultant, both in definition and in practice, underscore the diverse spectrum of expertise available in today's professional landscape. Each role, with its distinct operational, financial, and legal facets, offers unique value propositions, ensuring that organisations can access the right skill set and strategic guidance at the right time. For professionals considering the transition from contractor to consultant, the journey is not merely about changing designations but about evolving one's approach to problem-solving and value creation. As with any transformative path, open communication, clarity of purpose, and a genuine commitment to the client's success remain paramount. Whether you're an organisation seeking expertise or a professional charting your career path, understanding these roles' intricacies ensures more informed, impactful, and fulfilling engagements.

Ok, phew, we're there. It's a complex topic with no distinct answer. There is no silver bullet or right answer. The closing advice I offer my mentees is that whatever happens, professionalism matters. If you took on/ accepted an engagement as a contractor for a defined period and agreed on a rate, see it through first.

To the opening question, can a contractor become a consultant? Possibly, It's the only possible answer and I hope you understand why.

Rachael Evans MA, FCMI

12. In-house Knowledge Development and External Consultation: Impact on Organisational Growth and Value

Today, most organisations face the imperative of continually developing and augmenting their knowledge base to maintain competitiveness and drive innovation. Central to this endeavour is the decision between nurturing in-house expertise or engaging external consultants and specialists. This paper critically examines the value proposition of these contrasting approaches, analysing their respective contributions and drawbacks in terms of organisational growth and value creation. Through an integration of academic literature, including seminal works by Nonaka (1994), Penrose (1959), and others, along with practical examples from companies such as Google, Apple, NASA, and Nokia, this study offers an in depth exploration of the underlying dynamics at play. The factors considered include the retention of intellectual property, cultural alignment, cost-effectiveness, access to specialised expertise, objectivity, flexibility, and scalability.

The paper further discusses the challenges associated with each approach, such as limited perspectives, resource constraints, cost intensiveness, and potential knowledge drain. Concluding with a synthesis of insights, the paper posits that the choice between in-house development and external engagement is contingent upon a confluence of factors including strategic alignment, resources, and broader market dynamics. Additionally, it suggests that a hybrid approach, integrating elements of both strategies, may often offer an optimal balance for organisations navigating the intricate landscape of knowledge acquisition and development.

Introduction

In an era marked by rapid technological advancements, globalisation, and ever-evolving market dynamics, organisations are incessantly faced with critical decisions regarding the growth and development of their knowledge base. Two prevailing approaches are central to this discussion: the development and growth of in-house knowledge, and the engagement of external consultants and specialists. The choice between these approaches is not merely a tactical decision; rather, it holds profound implications for an organisation's innovation, adaptability, and competitive positioning. This paper explores the dichotomy between these strategies, examining the distinctive value propositions each offers, and investigating the implications for organisational growth and value creation.

Developing and Growing In-house Knowledge

Developing in-house knowledge involves cultivating and augmenting the skills, competencies, and intellectual capital of an organisation's existing workforce. This strategy is predicated on the belief that a knowledgeable and adept workforce can be a potent source of innovation and a cornerstone of competitive advantage (Grant, 1996). Activities such as training, mentorship, knowledge-sharing platforms, and continuous learning are integral components of this approach. Moreover, the retention of intellectual property, cultural alignment, and potential cost-effectiveness make it an attractive prospect for many organisations. However, it is imperative to consider the challenges and limitations inherent to this approach, including potential insularity, resource constraints, and the risk of stagnant innovation (Nonaka, 1994; Penrose, 1959).

Engaging External Consultants and Specialists

On the other hand, hiring external consultants and specialists often allows organisations to tap into a reservoir of specialised expertise and objectivity, which might not be available internally. This approach is especially valuable for addressing complex challenges, acquiring fresh perspectives, and navigating through transformative changes (McKenna, 1995). Additionally, the scalability and flexibility offered by this approach enable organisations to adeptly respond to fluctuating needs. However, engaging external expertise is not without its drawbacks, including the financial burden, potential knowledge and skills drain postengagement, and cultural misalignment (Biswas & Twitchell, 2002; David & Foray, 2003).

12. In-house Knowledge Development and External Consultation

Navigating the Trade-offs

Given that each approach carries its own set of advantages and disadvantages, it is vital for decision-makers to weigh the trade-offs. The decision matrix might include considerations such as the strategic importance of the knowledge in question, availability of resources, time constraints, and the long-term vision of the organisation. In some instances, a hybrid approach that combines elements of both strategies may provide an optimal balance. This paper delves into a detailed examination of the approaches, enriched with academic literature and practical examples. By providing insights into the distinct value propositions and associated trade-offs, this paper aspires to furnish organisational leaders with the analytical frameworks needed to make informed decisions that align with their strategic objectives and foster sustained growth and value creation.

Developing In-house Knowledge

The strategic development and management of knowledge have become critical factors for organisational success. One approach that organisations can adopt to leverage knowledge as a strategic asset is by developing and nurturing expertise within their workforce, known as in-house knowledge development. This encompasses a range of activities including training, upskilling, mentorship, and the creation of platforms for knowledge sharing and collaboration.

In-house knowledge development seeks to build a reservoir of skills, competencies, and intellectual capital that are tailored to the organisation's objectives and culture (Davenport & Prusak, 1998). This is based on the premise that an informed and skilled workforce is better equipped to innovate, make decisions, and contribute to the organisation's competitiveness and growth (Nonaka, 1994).

While developing in-house knowledge has its advantages, it is important to consider the intricate balance between benefits and drawbacks. In this section, we delve into the advantages of in-house knowledge development, such as the retention of intellectual property, cultural alignment, cost-effectiveness, responsiveness, and employee satisfaction. Furthermore, we explore the challenges that come with this approach, including limited perspectives, resource constraints, diminished external networks, and opportunity costs.

As we discuss these facets, it is important to recognize that the choice to invest in in-house knowledge development is contingent upon various factors including organisational goals, industry dynamics, and available resources. Through a balanced examination, this section aims to equip organisations with insights to make informed decisions regarding their knowledge development strategies.

Let's examine the advantages and disadvantages of developing in-house competencies:

The Advantages

1. **Retention of Intellectual Property**: The development of in-house expertise ensures that knowledge remains within the organisation (Nonaka, 1994). This is crucial for retaining intellectual property, which can be a source of sustainable competitive advantage. When employees develop novel solutions or innovations, the organisation retains exclusive rights to these developments. Furthermore, building on in-house knowledge creates a repository of organisational memory, which can be leveraged for future projects and innovations, thereby enhancing the organisation's ability to respond to market demands efficiently (Davenport & Prusak, 1998).

2. **Cultural Alignment**: Internal teams are generally more aligned with the organisation's culture, which can foster collaboration and improve decision-making (Schein, 1985). A strong organisational culture can facilitate knowledge sharing among employees, leading to a more informed and cohesive workforce (Cameron & Quinn, 2011). Moreover, employees who identify with the organisation's values and goals are likely to exhibit greater commitment and engagement, which ultimately contribute to enhanced performance and productivity (Kotter, 2008).

3. **Cost-effectiveness**: In the long-term, investing in employee development can prove to be more cost-effective as opposed to recurrent consulting fees (Becker, 1962). Building and maintaining in-house expertise might have a higher initial cost due to training and development, but over time, the organisation can reap the benefits of having a skilled workforce without the need for continuous external consultation. Furthermore, an internally developed workforce can provide a pool of talent for succession planning, reducing the costs associated with turnover and recruitment (Huselid, 1995).

4. **Responsiveness and Agility**: When expertise is developed in-house, organisations can be more responsive to changes and challenges. Internal teams are more likely to have a deep understanding of the business and its nuances. This allows for quicker decision making and an ability to adapt strategies or processes more rapidly compared to the lead time that might be needed when engaging external consultants (Teece, Pisano, & Shuen, 1997).

5. **Employee Satisfaction and Retention**: Investing in the development of in-house knowledge often results in increased employee satisfaction and retention rates (Harter, Schmidt, & Hayes, 2002). When employees feel that the organisation is invested in their growth and development, they are more likely to remain committed to the organisation. This reduces turnover costs and ensures continuity in knowledge and expertise.

The Disadvantages:

1. **Limited Perspective**: Relying solely on internal resources may limit exposure to diverse perspectives and approaches, potentially stifling innovation (Tushman & O'Reilly, 1996). When an organisation is heavily ingrained in its ways of thinking and operating, it can fall victim to what is known as the "not invented here" syndrome. This term reflects a mindset where internal teams are reluctant to adopt ideas or approaches that originated outside the organisation (Katz & Allen, 1982). Such a mindset can hinder the incorporation of new ideas and lead to stagnation. Moreover, the lack of diversity in perspectives might contribute to confirmation bias, where individuals seek or interpret information in ways that affirm their pre-existing beliefs, which can impede critical thinking and innovation (Nickerson, 1998).

2. **Resource Constraints**: The development of expertise requires a significant investment in time and resources, which may not always be feasible for the organisation (Penrose, 1959). Training and upskilling employees necessitate not only financial resources but also time, which is particularly challenging for organisations that need to respond swiftly to market demands. Additionally, the limited pool of talent within the organisation may result in over-reliance on a few experts. If these experts leave or are otherwise unavailable, the organisation could face knowledge gaps that hinder its ability to perform effectively (Droege & Hoobler, 2003).

3. **Diminished External Networks**: Focusing solely on in-house knowledge development may cause an organisation to lose out on establishing valuable networks with external experts and institutions (Powell, Koput & Smith-Doerr, 1996). Such networks can be crucial for staying abreast of industry trends, gaining access to cutting-edge research, and creating opportunities for collaboration.
4. **Opportunity Costs**: Investing heavily in in-house development may lead to opportunity costs, where resources allocated for this purpose cannot be used for other strategic initiatives (Dixit & Pindyck, 1994). For instance, capital invested in long-term employee development programs might have been used more effectively in market expansion or product development.

External Consultants and Specialists

In the quest for organisational growth and innovation, the engagement of external consultants and specialists emerges as a pivotal strategy. This approach entails bringing in experts from outside the organisation to provide insights, advice, and skills that may not be available within the internal talent pool. External consultants and specialists often come with a wealth of experience and a diverse knowledge base accrued from working with multiple clients across various industries. In this section, we delve into the intricacies of engaging external consultants and specialists, analysing the value proposition that this approach offers and evaluating how it can bolster or, in some instances, impede organisational growth and value creation.

Engaging external expertise is especially relevant in situations that demand highly specialised skills, an objective viewpoint, or rapid scaling of capabilities to address specific challenges. Moreover, in an age where technological advancements and market shifts occur at a breakneck pace, external consultants can provide the agility and acumen needed to keep abreast of these changes.

However, like any strategic choice, engaging external consultants and specialists comes with its own set of considerations and trade-offs. In this section, we will explore the advantages of this approach, such as expertise and specialisation, objective insights, and flexibility and scalability. Concurrently, we will examine the associated challenges, including cost intensiveness and potential knowledge drain. We will supplement our analysis

12. In-house Knowledge Development and External Consultation

with practical examples and academic references to provide a well-rounded perspective on the merits and drawbacks of this approach.

Let's look at the advantages and disadvantages of engaging with external specialists and consultants:

Advantages

1. **Expertise and Specialisation**: External consultants often possess specialised knowledge and skills that are unavailable in-house, which can be instrumental in solving complex problems (McKenna, 1995). Consultants usually have extensive experience across different industries and organisations, which enables them to bring best practices and innovations to the table. For example, a cybersecurity consulting firm could provide a wealth of expertise in network security and data protection that an internal IT department might lack. Additionally, consultants often have access to specialized tools and methodologies which can be utilized to bring efficiencies and add value to the projects they are engaged in (Biswas & Twitchell, 2002).

2. **Objective Insights**: Being external to the organisation, consultants are less likely to be influenced by internal politics or biases, thus providing a more objective perspective (Turner, 1982). This can be particularly valuable in situations where sensitive decisions or organisational changes are needed. For instance, in a restructuring scenario, an external consultant might be able to provide unbiased recommendations regarding workforce optimization, whereas an internal team might be influenced by personal relationships or departmental interests.

3. **Flexibility and Scalability**: Hiring external consultants can be easily scaled up or down as per the organisational needs without long-term commitments (Lacity, Khan, & Willcocks, 2009). This provides organisations with the flexibility to bring in expertise for specific projects or initiatives and then scale back once the objectives are achieved. This can be particularly useful for small and medium-sized enterprises (SMEs) which might not have the resources to maintain a full-time, specialized workforce.

4. **Speed and Efficiency**: Consultants can often hit the ground running and help to accelerate the timeline of projects or initiatives. Since they bring

in a wealth of experience and don't require the learning curve that internal employees might need, they can contribute to faster decision-making and execution (Christensen, Olesen & Kjar, 2005).

5. **Risk Mitigation**: Engaging external experts, particularly in areas like legal compliance, cybersecurity, or financial auditing, can help in mitigating risks. Consultants in these fields are usually well-versed with the regulatory environment and can guide organisations in ensuring adherence to legal and industry standards, thereby preventing costly penalties and damage to reputation (Taplin, Bent & Aeron-Thomas, 2006).

Disadvantages

1. **Cost Intensiveness**: Engaging external specialists can be financially burdensome, especially for small to medium-sized enterprises (Biswas & Twitchell, 2002). While consultants bring specialized knowledge and expertise, they often come at a premium. This cost not only includes their fees but may also encompass expenses related to travel, accommodation, and tools or resources they might require. For smaller organisations or those with constrained budgets, this can represent a significant outlay that may not necessarily yield a commensurate return on investment. Additionally, if the engagement is not clearly defined and managed, costs can escalate beyond initial estimates, creating financial strains (Engelhardt, Ragonesi & Williams, 2008).

2. **Knowledge Drain**: Post engagement, consultants may leave with valuable insights and learnings, creating a potential knowledge drain from the organisation (David & Foray, 2003). This is particularly problematic when external consultants develop bespoke solutions or strategies for the organisation but do not effectively transfer this knowledge to internal teams. Consequently, the organisation may become dependent on external expertise for the maintenance or further development of these solutions, which is not only costly but may also limit the organisation's ability to adapt and innovate independently (Argote & Ingram, 2000).

3. **Cultural Misalignment**: External consultants may not be fully attuned to the organisation's culture and values, which can create friction or misunderstandings with internal teams (Schein, 1985). This can affect the implementation of recommendations or strategies suggested by the

consultants. Employees may resist changes or new approaches if they perceive them as being imposed by external parties who do not understand the unique dynamics and values of the organisation.

4. **Lack of Ownership and Accountability**: Since consultants are not permanent members of the organisation, they may not have the same level of commitment and ownership over the projects they are involved in (Maister, 1997). This could lead to a focus on short-term results without considering the long-term implications. Furthermore, once the engagement ends, they are not accountable for the execution or the long-term success of their recommendations.

5. **Confidentiality Risks**: Bringing in external consultants may entail sharing sensitive information about the organisation's operations, finances, or strategies. This could potentially lead to confidentiality risks if the information is not handled appropriately or if non-disclosure agreements are not in place (Teece, 1986).

Examples

The following examples illustrate the different value propositions of developing in-house knowledge and hiring external consultants and specialists. In the case of Google, Apple, and Toyota, long-term investments in in-house capabilities have been crucial for innovation and competitive advantage. In contrast, NASA and Nokia's examples demonstrate how engaging with external experts can bring specialized knowledge and objectivity, helping to achieve strategic objectives more efficiently.

Developing and Growing In-house Knowledge

1. **Tech Giants like Google and Apple**: These companies are known for heavily investing in the development of in-house talent. Google, for instance, encourages employees to spend 20% of their time on side projects, which has led to the creation of products like Gmail and Google News (Mediratta & Bick, 2007). Apple, on the other hand, is known for its secrecy and highly integrated approach, where critical parts of product design and development are carried out in-house, thus retaining a competitive edge by tightly guarding its intellectual property (Lashinsky, 2011).

2. **Toyota Production System (TPS)**: Toyota's renowned production system is an example of building in-house expertise in manufacturing.

TPS, or Lean Manufacturing, was developed over decades and has allowed Toyota to achieve high levels of quality and efficiency (Liker, 2004). The culture and knowledge of TPS are deeply ingrained in Toyota's workforce, demonstrating the value of long-term investment in in-house development.

Hiring External Consultants and Specialists

1. **NASA and SpaceX Collaboration**: NASA's collaboration with SpaceX, an external private company, exemplifies the value of external expertise. By partnering with SpaceX for launching cargo and astronauts to the International Space Station, NASA leveraged SpaceX's specialized expertise in rocket manufacturing and launching at a fraction of the cost of developing similar capabilities in-house (Hitt, Ireland & Hoskisson, 2012).

2. **Nokia's Transformation**: In the early 2010s, Nokia, once a leader in mobile phones, faced a severe decline in its market share. Nokia engaged external consultants to help in the turnaround strategy. The consultants provided an outside perspective on the market trends and consumer preferences. This engagement played a key role in Nokia's strategic decision to sell its mobile phone division and successfully pivot to network infrastructure (Alcacer & Casadesus-Masanell, 2015).

Conclusion

In the contemporary business landscape, the acquisition and deployment of knowledge is paramount. Throughout this paper, we have meticulously examined the divergent approaches of developing and growing in-house knowledge versus engaging external consultants and specialists, elucidating the unique value propositions and trade-offs inherent in each. As the various academic references and practical examples substantiate, the choice between these approaches is complex and multifaceted, intimately intertwined with an organisation's objectives, resources, culture, and the milieu in which it operates.

The development of in-house knowledge, as evidenced by the examples of Google, Apple, and Toyota, has the potential to foster innovation, retain intellectual property, and engender a culture that is more conducive to collaboration and shared objectives. However, as discussed, this approach can be resource-intensive and may result in a somewhat myopic or insular perspective.

12. In-house Knowledge Development and External Consultation

Conversely, hiring external consultants and specialists, illustrated through the cases of NASA's collaboration with SpaceX and Nokia's transformation, offers the advantage of specialised expertise, objective insights, flexibility, and scalability. Yet, this approach is not without its pitfalls, including the financial burden, potential knowledge drain, and cultural misalignment

In navigating these complex trade-offs, it is incumbent upon organisational leaders to undertake a rigorous and thoughtful analysis. This involves assessing the alignment with strategic objectives, availability and allocation of resources, timelines, and the broader context in which the organisation operates. Moreover, it is essential to recognize that these approaches are not mutually exclusive. In many instances, a hybrid approach that judiciously combines elements of in-house development with external engagements may yield the best results.

As the business environment continues to evolve, it is imperative for organisations to remain agile and adaptable in their knowledge acquisition strategies. This paper underscores the importance of a nuanced understanding of the respective value propositions of developing in-house knowledge and engaging external consultants. By weighing the trade-offs and aligning decisions with strategic objectives, organisations can optimize their knowledge capital to drive innovation, competitive advantage, and sustainable growth.

In closing, as new methodologies and tools emerge, and as the global landscape continues to change, further research is encouraged to continually reassess and refine the strategies for knowledge acquisition and development in the organizational context.

References

Alcacer, J., & Casadesus-Masanell, R. (2015). Nokia's sharp turnaround since 2007. Strategy Science, 1(1), 36-47.

Argote, L., & Ingram, P. (2000). Knowledge transfer: A basis for compeve advantage in firms. Organizaonal behavior and human decision processes, 82(1), 150-169.

Becker, G. S. (1962). Investment in human capital: A theoretical analysis. Journal of Political Economy, 70(5, Part 2), 9-49.

Biswas, S., & Twitchell, D. P. (2002). Management consulting: A complete guide to the industry. John Wiley & Sons.

Cameron, K. S., & Quinn, R. E. (2011). Diagnosing and changing organizational culture: Based on the competing values framework. John Wiley & Sons.

Christensen, P. R., Olesen, M. H., & Kjar, J. S. (2005). The project model as an instrument for strengthening management and innovation. International Journal of Information Management, 25(4), 335-343.

Davenport, T. H., & Prusak, L. (1998). Working knowledge: How organizations manage what they know. Harvard Business Press.

David, P. A., & Foray, D. (2003). Economic fundamentals of the knowledge society. Policy Futures in Education, 1(1), 20-49.

Dixit, A. K., & Pindyck, R. S. (1994). Investment under uncertainty. Princeton University Press.

Droege, S. B., & Hoobler, J. M. (2003). Employee turnover and tacit knowledge diffusion: a network perspective. Journal of Managerial Issues, 176-193.

Engelhardt, S. E., Ragonesi, C., & Williams, T. (2008). Avoiding surprises: Using risk management to prevent scope creep. The Journal of Computing in Civil Engineering, 22(5), 311-315.

Garvin, D. A. (2000). Learning in action: A guide to putting the learning organization to work. Harvard Business Press.

Gerstner, L. V. (2002). Who says elephants can't dance?: Inside IBM's historic turnaround. Harper Collins.

Grant, R. M. (1996). Toward a knowledge-based theory of the firm. Strategic management journal, 17(S2), 109-122.

Harter, J. K., Schmidt, F. L., & Hayes, T. L. (2002). Business-unit-level relationship between employee satisfaction, employee engagement, and business outcomes: a meta-analysis. Journal of Applied Psychology, 87(2), 268.

Hitt, M. A., Ireland, R. D., & Hoskisson, R. E. (2012). Strategic management cases: competitiveness and globalization. Cengage Learning. Huselid, M. A. (1995). The impact of human resource management practices on turnover, productivity, and corporate financial performance. Academy of Management Journal, 38(3), 635-672.

Katz, R., & Allen, T. J. (1982). Investigating the Not Invented Here (NIH) syndrome: A look at the performance, tenure, and communication patterns of 50 R & D Project Groups. R&D Management, 12(1), 7-20.

Kotter, J. P. (2008). Corporate culture and performance. Simon and Schuster.

Lacity, M. C., Khan, S. A., & Willcocks, L. P. (2009). A review of the IT outsourcing literature: Insights for practice. Journal of Strategic Information Systems, 18(3), 130-146.

Lashinsky, A. (2011). Inside Apple: How America's Most Admired--and Secretive--Company Really Works. Hachette UK.

Liker, J. K. (2004). The Toyota way: 14 management principles from the world's greatest manufacturer. McGraw-Hill.

Maister, D. H. (1997). *True professionalism: The courage to care about your people, your clients, and your career.* Simon and Schuster.

McKenna, C. D. (1995). The origins of modern management consulting. *Business and Economic History, 24(1),* 51-58.

Mediratta, B., & Bick, G. (2007). The Google Way: Give Engineers Room. *The New York Times,* 21.

Nickerson, R. S. (1998). Confirmation bias: A ubiquitous phenomenon in many guises. *Review of General Psychology, 2(2),* 175-220.

Nonaka, I. (1994). A dynamic theory of organizational knowledge creation. *Organization Science, 5(1),* 14-37.

Penrose, E. T. (1959). *The theory of the growth of the firm.* Oxford University Press.

Pfeffer, J. (1994). *Competitive advantage through people: Unleashing the power of the workforce.* Harvard Business Press.

Powell, W. W., Koput, K. W., & Smith-Doerr, L. (1996). Interorganizational collaboration and the locus of innovation: Networks of learning in biotechnology. *Administrative Science Quarterly, 41 (1),* 116-145.

Schein, E. H. (1985). *Organizational culture and leadership.* Jossey-Bass.

Taplin, R., Bent, D., & Aeron-Thomas, D. (2006). Developing a risk management process for a road construction project. *Construction Management and Economics, 24(4),* 407-413.

Teece, D. J. (1986). Profiting from technological innovation: Implications for integration, collaboration, licensing and public policy. *Research policy, 15(6),* 285-305.

Teece, D. J., Pisano, G., & Shuen, A. (1997). Dynamic capabilities and strategic management. *Strategic Management Journal, 18(7),* 509-533.

Tushman, M. L., & O'Reilly, C. A. (1996). Ambidextrous organizations: Managing evolutionary and revolutionary change. *California Management Review, 38(4),* 8-30.

Turner, A. N. (1982). Consulting is more than giving advice. *Harvard Business Review, 60(5),* 120-129.

Rachael Evans MA, FCMI

13. The Implication of Military Management Techniques for the Commercial Sector: A Comparative Study

The business landscape has become increasingly competitive and volatile, necessitating robust and efficient management strategies. In this regard, the military management models of the UK and the US hold substantial insights for the civilian business world. This paper aims to explore what the commercial sector can gain from studying and implementing military management techniques, highlighting the key differences between the two models, and providing a roadmap for commercial organisations to adopt military-inspired operating models.

Introducton

The military, both in the UK and the US, represents an embodiment of crucial attributes that are essential for success in any organisation: discipline, leadership, strategic planning, and operaonal efficiency. These aributes have been well-documented and observed in numerous studies and contexts (Hannah, Uhl-Bien, Avolio, & Cavarrea, 2009). Whilst not all are comfortable or agree with the existence of military forces and the role they play in society; we should not dismiss their management techniques as there is much we can observe and leverage.

Discipline goes beyond mere obedience to orders. It entails the inculcaon of a sense of responsibility, adherence to set procedures, punctuality, and reliability. The value of discipline in the business world is equally significant. A disciplined workforce is likely to be more efficient, effecve, and less prone to errors, leading to enhanced producvity and competitiveness.

Leadership within the military structure is a crical factor in achieving organisaonal goals and mission success. Military leadership models emphasise the importance of communicaon, teamwork, adaptability, and decision-making under pressure. By studying and implemenng these leadership principles, businesses can culvate strong leaders who can guide their teams through uncertainty and challenges, fostering resilience and adaptability in the face of change.

Strategic planning involves careful, detailed, and oen long-term planning to achieve the desired objecves. This planning includes analysis of potenal threats and opportunies, evaluaon of resources, conngency planning, and connuous reassessment. By applying these strategic planning techniques, businesses can be better prepared to navigate the competitive business landscape, seizing opportunities while mitigating risks.

Operational efficiency refers to the opmal use of resources to achieve mission objectives. The military consistently works on reducing wastage, streamlining processes, and enhancing coordination among different units to maximise operational efficiency. This focus on efficiency can be beneficial for businesses that aim to reduce costs, improve service delivery, and maximise value for stakeholders. The management models used by the UK and US military are thus a rich source of insights for commercial organisations. They provide tangible and effective examples of how discipline, leadership, strategic planning, and operational efficiency can be nurtured and implemented to enhance organisational performance. Integrating these principles into civilian businesses' operating models can provide them with a competitive advantage, promoting a more disciplined, strategically focused, and efficient operation. The objective of this paper is to provide a deeper understanding of the intersection between military principles and business operations, ultimately showing how military techniques can offer fresh perspectives and tools for the civilian business world.

The Value of Military Management Techniques in Civilian Business

Over the years, the military has been recognised for its ability to operate under volatile, uncertain, complex, and ambiguous conditions, which is not too different from today's business environment. Thus, it's worth exploring how military management techniques can provide value to civilian businesses. This section delves into the essence of military management strategies and their potential benefits to the commercial sector. From crisis management and leadership development to strategic formulation, together we will unpack how these practices, formed within a military context, can help businesses become more resilient, adaptive, and effective in their operations.

Crisis Management

One of the standout features of military organisations is their proficiency in managing crises. Due to the inherently high-risk nature of military operations, they have developed sophisticated strategies and protocols to handle unexpected and challenging situations.

Firstly, military organisations prioritise planning and preparation in their crisis management approach. They invest significant time and resources in developing detailed contingency plans, outlining the necessary steps to take under various crisis scenarios. This proactive approach allows them to quickly identify the best course of action when a crisis occurs (Boin & Hart, 2007).

Moreover, the military practices regular drills and exercises to ensure that all personnel understand their roles and responsibilities during a crisis, fostering a level of readiness and adaptability that is crucial in crisis situations (Pfaff & Snook, 2002). This aspect of "trained readiness" is a critical component that businesses can integrate into their own crisis management models.

Communication is another key aspect of military crisis management. Military organisations prioritise clear, concise, and effective communication during crises to ensure that everyone is informed and aligned on the response strategy (U.S. Army, 2019). Businesses can learn from this by developing their own crisis communication plans and training their personnel in effective crisis communication.

In addition, military organisations also focus on maintaining operational continuity even in the face of crises. They have systems in place to ensure the continuity of operations, from alternative lines of supply to backup systems for essential functions (Boin & Hart, 2007). Businesses can apply this principle by developing their own business continuity plans, ensuring that they can continue to deliver their products or services even under crisis conditions.

Businesses can learn a lot about crisis management from military organisations. By incorporating military-style crisis management techniques into their own models – from proactive planning and preparation, regular drills and training, effective crisis communication, to operational continuity plans – businesses can significantly enhance their ability to handle crises, reduce potential losses, and maintain the trust of their stakeholders.

Human Resource Development

The military's approach to leadership development offers valuable insights for businesses. By their very nature, military organisations require effective leadership at all levels. This is achieved through a structured and consistent leadership development process.

Firstly, military organisations emphasise character development alongside technical skills. They recognise that good leaders require both professional competence and moral integrity. Leaders are expected to model values such as loyalty, duty, respect, selfless service, honour, integrity, and personal courage (U.S. Army, 2012). In the business context, leaders who exhibit strong character can inspire their teams, build trust, and contribute to a positive organisational culture.

Secondly, military organisations provide continual leadership training and education. This training includes practical exercises, simulations, and theoretical studies. By continually refining and expanding their leadership skills, military leaders are better prepared to adapt to changing circumstances and make effective decisions under pressure (Dixon & Westbrook, 2015).

Businesses can adopt a similar approach by investing in ongoing leadership development programs for their employees.

Finally, the military offers ample opportunities for individuals to practice leadership. From leading small teams to commanding entire units, military personnel gain practical leadership experience in various contexts and levels. This experiential learning is invaluable in developing effective leaders (Dixon & Westbrook, 2015). Businesses can take and apply this principle by providing their employees with opportunities to lead projects, teams, or initiatives.

Strategic Formulation

The strategic formulation in the military involves a thorough and deliberate planning process. Military organisations analyse their operational environment, assess their capabilities, and plan their operations to achieve their objectives while minimising risks (Department of the Army, 2019).

This process starts with a comprehensive environmental analysis. Military organisations gather and analyse information about potential threats, allies, terrain, and other factors that may influence their operations. This rigorous analysis enables them to understand their operational environment and make informed decisions (Department of the Army, 2019). Businesses can apply this principle by conducting thorough market research and competitive analysis.

Next, military organisations assess their own capabilities. They evaluate their personnel, equipment, and other resources to identify their strengths and weaknesses. This self assessment helps them allocate resources effectively and identify areas for improvement (Department of the Army, 2019). Similarly, businesses can conduct a SWOT analysis (Strengths, Weaknesses, Opportunities, and Threats) to understand their own capabilities and how they can leverage them in their strategic planning.

Lastly, military organisations develop detailed operation plans based on their environmental analysis and self-assessment. These plans outline their strategy for achieving their objectives, including contingency plans for potential risks and challenges (Department of the Army, 2019). In the business context, this corresponds to the development of a strategic business plan that guides the organisation's efforts to achieve its goals.

The Differences between Commercial and Military Management Models

Despite the substantial applicability of military management techniques to the commercial sector, it's crucial to acknowledge the inherent differences between these two arenas. The disparate operational environments, primary objectives, and structural systems give rise to unique management models within each. As I delve into these differences, I hope to provide a nuanced understanding of both commercial and military management models, with a particular emphasis on UK and US military organisations. This comprehension is pivotal, as it will help to delineate where commercial businesses could reap the benefits of integrating military practices, as well as the necessary adaptations for a successful transition.

The military's primary objective is mission accomplishment, which often involves life-and death scenarios and requires swift, decisive action. Its management model, therefore, prioritises the chain of command, unity of effort, and leadership development (Hughes et al., 2012). This model fosters discipline, efficiency, and cohesion, enabling military units to perform effectively under high-pressure circumstances and navigate complex operational environments. Specifically, UK and US military organisations manifest these priorities through hierarchical structures, clear lines of command, rigorous training programs, and well-defined operational procedures (UK Ministry of Defence, 2010; US Department of Defense, 2015).

In contrast, the commercial sector is driven by a myriad of objectives, including maximising profit, fostering innovation, satisfying customers, and expanding their market share (Drucker, 2007). As a result, commercial management models typically emphasise strategic planning, resource allocation, competitive analysis, customer relationship management, and innovation. These models create an environment that encourages creativity, adaptability, and customer-centricity, enabling businesses to thrive in a highly competitive and everevolving marketplace.

Commercial enterprises also contend with different regulatory frameworks, stakeholder expectations, and market dynamics compared to military organisations. These factors further differentiate the commercial management model and shape its strategies, structures, and operations.

While these differences are significant, they don't negate the value that each sector can offer the other. Rather, they highlight the need for careful

13. The Implications of Military Management Techniques

consideration and adaptation when transferring practices from one context to the other. By understanding the distinct features and mechanisms of these management models, businesses can better identify which military practices can be beneficially incorporated into their operations and how to adapt them to suit their specific needs and realities.

Adopting Military-Inspired Operating Models in Commercial Organisations

While it's insightful to understand the potential benefits and differences between military and commercial management models, it's equally crucial to examine how civilian businesses can practically incorporate military-inspired operating models. This section delves into the process of adopting these practices, providing a pragmatic roadmap for commercial organisations interested in leveraging the benefits of military management techniques. From leadership development and crisis management to communication and decision-making, we'll explore a range of strategies that can be adopted and adapted to suit each organisation's unique context. I'll also discuss the possible challenges that may arise during this transformation and suggest ways to mitigate them. By the end of this section, readers should have an insight into how they can incorporate military-inspired practices into their operating models, bolstering their capacity for resilience, agility, and growth.

Leadership Development

Commercial organisations can adopt military-inspired leadership development techniques by first focusing on character development in their leaders. This could be achieved through workshops, training programs, or coaching sessions that help leaders to understand and exemplify the organisation's core values (Bungay, 2011).

Secondly, ongoing leadership training and education can be integrated into the organisational culture. Businesses can create an environment that values continuous learning and improvement. This might involve in-house training sessions, online courses, mentoring programs, or opportunities to attend relevant conferences or seminars.

Finally, offering leadership opportunities at all levels of the organisation can help to cultivate future leaders. For instance, junior employees could be given the chance to lead small projects, while more senior personnel might take charge of larger initiatives. This hands-on leadership experience, complemented by feedback and reflection, can accelerate leadership development (Hannah, Avolio, Luthans, & Harms, 2008).

Crisis Management

Commercial organisations can apply military crisis management techniques by investing in contingency planning. Businesses can create detailed plans outlining the steps to take under various crisis scenarios, which could range from data breaches to natural disasters (Boin, McConnell, & Hart, 2008)

Regular crisis drills can also be beneficial. These exercises can help employees understand their roles during a crisis, ensuring that the organisation can respond effectively when a real crisis occurs.

Finally, organisations can improve their crisis communication by training leaders and employees in effective communication techniques and developing a clear crisis communication plan. This plan should outline how information will be communicated during a crisis, to whom, and by whom (Coombs, 2014).

Strategic Formulation

Businesses looking to adopt military strategic formulation techniques could begin by prioritising comprehensive market research and competitor analysis. These initiatives may include various methods such as customer surveys to gather direct feedback, focus groups to gain deeper insights, analysis of market trends to understand larger industry dynamics, and profiling of competitors to benchmark performance and identify areas of differentiation.

In addition to external analysis, businesses should also undertake an introspective evaluation of their own capabilities. Techniques like SWOT analysis, which considers the organisation's strengths, weaknesses, opportunities, and threats, can prove valuable here. This self-assessment shouldn't be limited to tangible resources, like financial capacity or physical assets. It should also factor in intangible resources, such as the skills of employees or the value of the brand's reputation.

Upon collating and synthesising the insights from both external and internal analyses, the organisation can then proceed to develop a strategic business plan. This plan should articulate the organisation's goals and map out the strategies to realise them. Importantly, it should also account for potential risks and incorporate contingency plans to mitigate these. This comprehensive and forward-looking approach is a defining characteristic of military strategic formulation and can serve to enhance the strategic planning of commercial businesses (Hitt, Ireland, & Hoskisson, 2017).

Operational Efficiency

Companies can learn from military operational efficiency by continually seeking ways to reduce waste and streamline processes. Techniques like lean management or Six Sigma, which have been successfully implemented in various industries, could be useful here (Antony, 2014).

Organisations can also enhance coordination among different departments or teams, ensuring that everyone is aligned towards the organisation's objectives. This could involve regular inter-departmental meetings, collaborative tools, or team-building activities.

Finally, businesses can establish systems to ensure operational continuity. This might involve having alternative suppliers, backup systems for critical operations, or insurance coverage for potential business disruptions (Sullivan-Taylor & Branicki, 2011).

Conclusion

Military management techniques provide a wealth of insights and practices that can be adopted and adapted by the commercial sector to drive success. Our exploration of the areas of crisis management, leadership development, strategic formulation, and operational efficiency underscores the unique lessons the military offers in these domains. These lessons are exemplified in the robust and meticulous planning processes, the emphasis on character and continuous learning in leadership development, the strategies for maintaining operational efficiency, and the readiness and resilience inherent in crisis management.

However, integrating military techniques into a civilian business context should not be done in an uncritical or wholesale manner. It's vital to recognise the differing environments and objectives between the military and commercial sectors. While the military operates with a command-and-control style, businesses may function better with a more participative and collaborative style. Recognising these differences allows businesses to modify and adapt military techniques to suit their own needs and realities.

Moreover, the adoption of these military management techniques should be a well-thought-out process. It requires not only a clear understanding of these techniques but also a comprehensive plan for their implementation. By investing in leadership development programs, crafting detailed crisis management plans, carrying out thorough strategic formulations, and focusing on operational efficiency, businesses can incorporate the strengths of the military management model into their operations.

It is my hope that this exploration acts as a catalyst for further research and discussion on this topic. By learning from each other, the military and commercial sectors can continue to innovate and adapt, fostering a symbiosis that enhances both domains. It is not about militarising the commercial sector, but about taking the best from each model to build resilient, efficient, and successful organisations that can navigate the complexities and challenges of the 21st-century business landscape.

References & Further Reading

Antony, J. (2014). *Driving operaonal excellence: successful lean six sigma secrets to improve the boom line.* McGraw Hill Professional.

Boin, A., & Hart, P. (2007). *The Crisis Approach.* In H. Rodríguez, E. Quarantelli, & R. Dynes (Eds.), Handbook of Disaster Research (pp. 42-54). Springer.

Boin, A., McConnell, A., & Hart, P. T. (2008). *Governing aer crisis: The polics of invesgaon, accountability and learning.* Cambridge University Press.

Bungay, S. (2011). *The Art of Acon: How Leaders Close the Gaps between Plans, Acons and Results.* Nicholas Brealey Publishing.

Coombs, W. T. (2014). *Ongoing crisis communicaon: Planning, managing, and responding.* Sage Publicaons.

Department of the Army. (2019). *Army Doctrine Publicaon 5-0, The Operaons Process.* U.S. Government Publishing Office.

Dixon, G., & Westbrook, J. (2015). *Military experience and levels of stress and coping in police officers. Internaonal Journal of Emergency Mental Health and Human Resilience, 17(2),* 661-667.

Drucker, P. (2007). *The Pracce of Management.* Harper & Brothers.

Hannah, S. T., Uhl-Bien, M., Avolio, B. J., & Cavarrea, F. L. (2009). *A framework for examining leadership in extreme contexts. The Leadership Quarterly, 20(6),* 897-919.

Hannah, S. T., Avolio, B. J., Luthans, F., & Harms, P. D. (2008). *Leadership efficacy: Review and future direcons. The Leadership Quarterly, 19(5),* 669-692.

Hitt, M. A., Ireland, R. D., & Hoskisson, R. E. (2017). *Strategic management: concepts and cases: compeveness and globalizaon.* Cengage Learning.

13. The Implications of Military Management Techniques

Hughes, R. L., Ginne, R. C., & Curphy, G. J. (2012). *Leadership: Enhancing the lessons of experience*. McGraw-Hill.

Pfaff, R., & Snook, S. (2002). The Effects of Planning on Decision-Making Processes and Performance: An Empirical Study of U.S. Army Command and Control Teams. *Journal of Conngencies and Crisis Management, 10*(3), 151-162.

Sullivan-Taylor, B., & Branicki, L. (2011). Creang resilient SMEs: why one size might not fit all. *Internaonal Journal of Producon Research, 49*(18), 5565-5579.

UK Ministry of Defence (2010). *The Defence Manual of Security*. Crown Copyright.

UK Ministry of Defence. (2010). *Joint Doctrine Publicaon 0-01, UK Defence Doctrine*. Ministry of Defence.

U.S. Army. (2019). *Field Manual 6-0, Commander and Staff Organisaon and Operaons*. U.S. Government Publishing Office.

U.S. Army. (2012). *Army Doctrine Publicaon 6-22, Army Leadership*. U.S. Government Publishing Office.

US Department of Defense (2015). *Joint Publicaon 3-0, Joint Operaons*. US Government Prinng Office.

US Department of Defense. (2015). *Joint Publicaon 1, Doctrine for the Armed Forces of the United States*. US Government Publishing Office.

Whington, R. (2001). *What is strategy - and does it maer?* Thomson Learning.

Rachael Evans MA, FCMI

14. Navigating Unresolved Non-Performing Peer Issues: Handling, Raising Attention, and Implementing Strategies

Handling a non-performing peer at work can be a difficult and frustrating experience, especially when management is reluctant to address the issue. Unresolved underperformance can lead to decreased productivity, strained team dynamics, and increased stress for other team members. In this article, I'll present a number of techniques to handle the situation, raise attention to the problem, and implement strategies to minimise the impact when management fails to resolve the issue.

To better assist, I have employed a list-oriented approach that prioritises the steps and actions you may consider for each category. This format will facilitate a clear understanding and help you effectively implement the suggested strategies.

Focus on Your Own Performance

Dealing with a non-performing peer can be challenging, but it's crucial to remain focused on your own performance and professional growth. By excelling in your work and demonstrating your commitment to the team's success, you can continue to make a positive impact on your team and organisation. Here are some tips to maintain focus and drive success in your own performance:

- **Set Personal Goals**: Establish clear and measurable goals for your own performance, ensuring that they align with your team's objectives and your organisation's broader goals. Regularly review and adjust these goals as needed to stay on track.
- **Prioritise Tasks**: Effectively manage your time by prioritising tasks based on their importance and deadlines. This will help you stay focused on your work, even in the face of challenges posed by a non-performing colleague.
- **Maintain a Positive Attitude**: Foster a positive mindset by focusing on your accomplishments and the aspects of your work that you enjoy. Recognise that setbacks and challenges are part of any work environment and maintain resilience in the face of adversity.
- **Seek Professional Development Opportunities**: Actively pursue opportunities to expand your skills and knowledge, whether through training, workshops, or self-directed learning. This will not only improve your performance but also demonstrate your commitment to personal growth and the success of your team.
- **Communicate Your Achievements**: Regularly update your manager and teammates on your progress and accomplishments. This will help reinforce your value to the team and showcase your dedication to the team's success.
- **Establish Boundaries**: While it's essential to be supportive of your colleagues, ensure that you establish boundaries to protect your own workload and well-being. Politely decline requests that may stretch your capacity or distract you from your priorities.

By focusing on your own performance and taking proactive steps to excel in your work, you can continue to make a positive impact on your team and organisation, even when dealing with a non-performing peer. Maintaining your commitment to the team's success and your own professional growth can help mitigate the challenges posed by a non-performing colleague and foster a more productive work environment.

Maintain Open Communication

Maintaining open communication with a non-performing colleague is a crucial step in addressing the issue and fostering a positive working relationship.

14. Navigating Unresolved Non-Performing Peer Issues

When engaging in conversations with your peer, consider the following guidelines to ensure a constructive and non-confrontational approach:

- **Use "I" Statements**: Frame your concerns using "I" statements to express how the situation affects you and your work, rather than assigning blame. For example, say "I've noticed that I've had to take on extra tasks because the deadlines were missed," instead of "You always miss deadlines."

- **Focus on Work-Related Issues**: Keep the conversation focused on specific work-related issues and avoid discussing personal attributes that may be unrelated to job performance. This approach helps to maintain professionalism and prevents the conversation from becoming personal or accusatory.

- **Encourage Open Dialogue**: Invite your colleague to share their perspective on the situation and any challenges they might be experiencing. This open dialogue can help identify underlying issues and provide insights into potential solutions.

By maintaining open communication and addressing your concerns in a constructive, nonconfrontational manner, you can create an environment that fosters collaboration and problem-solving, ultimately contributing to a more productive and harmonious workplace.

Document the Impact

Documenting the impact of your colleague's underperformance is a critical step in building a case for management intervention or HR involvement. Proper documentation ensures that your concerns are substantiated by tangible evidence and provides a clear picture of the issues at hand. Here's how to effectively record the impact of your colleague's underperformance:

- Maintain a Detailed Log: Create a log or journal where you can document specific instances of underperformance, such as missed deadlines, incomplete tasks, errors, or other consequences. Be sure to include dates, project details, and any communication or attempts made to address the issue with your colleague.

- **Quantify the Impact**: Whenever possible, quantify the impact of your colleague's underperformance. For example, indicate the number of hours you or other team members had to spend to compensate for the incomplete tasks, the financial costs incurred due to delays or errors, or the number of clients affected by the underperformance.

- **Track Project Timelines**: Document any instances where your colleague's underperformance caused delays or disruptions to project timelines. Include details of the specific tasks, the extent of the delay, and any cascading effects on other team members or project milestones.
- **Highlight Effects on Team Morale**: Note any instances where the underperformance has led to a decline in team morale or increased tension among team members. Describe how the situation has impacted the overall work environment and the relationships between colleagues.
- **Compile Correspondence**: Gather any relevant email correspondence, meeting notes, or performance reviews that highlight the underperformance issues and your attempts to address them. This information can help demonstrate your proactive efforts to resolve the situation.
- **Maintain Confidentiality**: Ensure that your documentation is stored securely and only shared with appropriate parties, such as your manager or HR. Respect your colleague's privacy by refraining from sharing the information with others who are not directly involved in the resolution process.
- **Be Objective and Factual**: When documenting the impact of your colleague's underperformance, maintain a professional and objective tone. Stick to the facts and avoid using emotionally charged language or expressing personal opinions.

In thoroughly documenting the impact of your colleague's underperformance, you can present a well-substantiated case when raising your concerns with higher levels of management or HR. This documentation will serve as valuable evidence to support your claims and help facilitate a more effective resolution process.

Seek Allies

Building a united front with other team members who share your concerns about a nonperforming colleague can strengthen your case and highlight the urgency of addressing the issue. By working together, you can demonstrate the seriousness of the problem and the need for management intervention. Here are some steps to effectively involve your teammates and build a united front:

- **Identify Concerned Teammates**: Discreetly approach colleagues who may have experienced similar issues with the non-performing peer or have expressed concerns about their performance. Gauge their level of interest in addressing the issue and ensure they share your goal of resolving the problem professionally.

- **Share Experiences and Documentations**: Exchange experiences, insights, and any documentation you and your teammates have gathered regarding the underperformance. This collaborative approach can provide a more comprehensive understanding of the situation and strengthen your collective case.

- **Establish a Common Goal**: Agree on a common goal that focuses on improving the overall team performance and addressing the specific issues caused by the non-performing colleague. Emphasise the importance of finding a resolution that benefits everyone, including the underperforming peer, by helping them improve and contribute positively to the team.

- **Develop a Joint Action Plan**: Collaborate with your teammates to develop a joint action plan for addressing the issue. This plan may include speaking to the underperforming colleague, escalating the issue to management, or proposing solutions to improve performance.

- **Present a United Front**: When raising the issue with management or HR, present a united front to demonstrate the collective concern and the need for intervention. Ensure that each team member involved articulates their perspective and shares their experiences, highlighting the impact of the underperformance on the entire team.

- **Maintain Professionalism**: Throughout the process, maintain professionalism and avoid engaging in gossip or personal attacks. Focus on work-related issues and ensure that your collective efforts aim to improve the situation rather than discredit the non-performing colleague.

- **Support Each Other**: Recognise that addressing a non-performing peer can be a stressful and challenging experience. Provide support and encouragement to your teammates, and work together to maintain a positive and collaborative work environment.

By involving other team members who share your concerns and presenting a united front, you can effectively demonstrate the seriousness of the problem and the need for management intervention. This collaborative approach can help facilitate a resolution that benefits the entire team and fosters a more productive and harmonious workplace.

Escalate the Issue

If your direct manager fails to address the issue of a non-performing colleague, it may become necessary to escalate the matter to a higher level of management or your company's human resources department. Approaching this escalation professionally and effectively is crucial to ensure the problem is adequately addressed. Here are some steps to follow when escalating the issue:

- **Review Company Policies**: Familiarise yourself with your organisation's policies and procedures regarding performance management and escalation processes. Ensure that you follow the appropriate steps and guidelines outlined by your company.
- **Prepare Documentation**: Organise your collected documentation, including logs of incidents, missed deadlines, the impact on productivity, and any attempts made to address the issue informally. This evidence will help support your claims and demonstrate the need for action.
- **Choose the Appropriate Channel**: Determine the most appropriate person or department to escalate the issue to, whether it be a higher-level manager, a department head, or the human resources department. Ensure that you respect the hierarchy and reporting lines within your organisation.
- **Request a Meeting**: Formally request a meeting with the appropriate party to discuss the issue. Provide a brief overview of your concerns and explain that you've attempted to address the matter with your direct manager but have not seen any resolution.

- **Present Your Case Professionally**: During the meeting, present your documented evidence in a clear and concise manner, focusing on the impact of the underperformance on the team and the steps you've taken to address the issue informally. Maintain a professional tone and avoid making personal attacks or expressing frustration.
- **Offer Solutions**: Come prepared with potential solutions or recommendations for addressing the issue. This may include additional training, closer supervision, or a performance improvement plan for your non-performing colleague. Demonstrating a proactive approach can help facilitate a resolution.
- **Establish a Follow-Up Plan**: End the meeting by discussing the next steps and agreeing on a timeline for action. Request updates on the progress of the issue and, if appropriate, schedule a follow-up meeting to assess the situation after a reasonable period.
- **Maintain Confidentiality**: Throughout the escalation process, be mindful of your colleague's privacy and avoid discussing the issue with others who are not directly involved in the resolution process.

By escalating the issue to a higher level of management or your company's human resources department professionally and effectively, you increase the likelihood of achieving a resolution. Presenting documented evidence of the impact on the team and highlighting the steps you've taken to address the issue informally demonstrates your commitment to finding a solution that benefits both the non-performing colleague and the entire team.

Consider Alternative Options

In cases where the issue with a non-performing peer remains unresolved despite your efforts, it's essential to evaluate your options within the organisation to protect your well-being and professional growth. One viable option to consider is exploring opportunities for an internal transfer. By doing so, you may find a better-suited team or project that allows you to thrive and contribute effectively to the company's success. Begin by researching available positions, talking to colleagues from other departments, or networking with managers who might have opportunities that align with your skills and interests. It's important to weigh the pros and cons of making a move, considering factors such as career advancement, personal development, and work-life balance. If you find an opportunity that interests you, discuss the possibility of transferring with your manager or human resources department, expressing your desire to contribute more effectively to the organisation in a new role or team. Emphasise your commitment to the company and your eagerness to grow professionally. By carefully evaluating your options and making a strategic move within the organisation, you can potentially find a more supportive and productive work environment, allowing you to excel in your career and overcome the challenges posed by a non-performing colleague.

In Closing

Dealing with a non-performing peer at work can be challenging, especially when management is reluctant to address the issue. By taking proactive steps such as maintaining open communication, documenting the impact of their underperformance, collaborating with concerned team members, and escalating the issue professionally, you can work towards finding a resolution. Additionally, focusing on your own performance and professional growth can help you continue to make a positive impact on your team and organisation. If the issue remains unresolved, carefully evaluate your options within the organisation, explore internal transfer opportunities, or discuss the possibility of moving to a different team or project. By adopting a strategic approach and taking control of your own career, you can overcome the challenges posed by a non-performing colleague and foster a more productive and supportive work environment.

Rachael Evans MA, FCMI

15. The Reluctant Leader: Adapting Technical Skills to a Management Role

Individual contributors and technicians who excel in their roles are often promoted to management positions. These new leaders may find themselves in unfamiliar territory, facing challenges such as managing people, products, and customers. This paper aims to explore strategies for adapting technical skills to management roles while retaining core skills, enthusiasm, and passion. Furthermore, the potential consequences of placing technicians in management roles without adequate training or support are discussed.

The promotion of high-performing individual contributors to management positions is a common practice in organisations (Benson, 2021). However, many technicians or individual contributors may lack the necessary skills and experience to excel in these new roles, which can lead to ineffective leadership and negative consequences for both the individuals and the organisations they serve (Kahnweiler, 2018). This paper discusses the process of adapting technical skills to management roles and the potential pitfalls of placing unprepared technicians in these positions.

Adapting Technical Skills to Management Roles

One of the primary challenges technicians faces when transitioning to management roles is the shift from focusing on technical work to managing people (Benson, 2021). To address the challenge of shifting focus from technical work to managing people, technicians should consider the following expanded strategies:

- Develop emotional intelligence (EI) to better understand, empathise, and communicate with team members (Goleman, 2004).
  - Practice self-awareness by identifying personal emotions, strengths, and weaknesses.
  - Enhance self-regulation by managing emotions and impulses effectively.
  - Improve social awareness by recognising and understanding the emotions of others.
  - Develop relationship management skills by building rapport, resolving conflicts, and fostering collaboration.
- Learn to delegate tasks effectively to empower team members and create a sense of ownership (HBR, 2021).
  - Identify the strengths and capabilities of team members to assign tasks that align with their skills.
  - Provide clear instructions and expectations, while allowing for autonomy and creativity.
  - Establish a system for tracking progress and providing feedback.
  - Encourage team members to take initiative and make decisions within their areas of responsibility.
- Develop coaching and mentoring skills to support and develop the potential of team members (Bungay Stanier, 2016).
  - Adopt a coaching mindset by asking open-ended questions, listening actively, and providing guidance rather than dictating solutions.
  - Create a supportive environment where team members feel comfortable discussing challenges, successes, and areas for improvement.
  - Offer constructive feedback that focuses on growth and learning.
  - Share personal experiences and lessons learned to help team members navigate their career development.
- Foster a sense of belonging and inclusivity within the team (Catalyst, 2020).

15. The Reluctant Leader

- Encourage open communication and active listening among team members to build trust and understanding.
- Value and appreciate the diverse perspectives and experiences of team members, recognising that diversity leads to better decision-making and problem-solving.
- Implement inclusive practices such as equitable workload distribution, transparent decision-making processes, and recognition of individual contributions.

• Adapt leadership style to the needs of the team (Goleman, 2000).
- Develop a range of leadership styles, such as authoritative, democratic, coaching, and affiliative, to adapt to different situations and team members' needs.
- Regularly assess the team's dynamics, strengths, and areas for improvement to determine the most effective leadership approach.
- Be open to feedback and willing to adjust leadership style as needed to support the team's growth and success.

By implementing these expanded strategies, technicians can successfully adapt their skills to manage people effectively and foster a positive, productive work environment.

Managing Products

As managers, technicians need to oversee the development and execution of products effectively. The following expanded strategies can help technicians enhance their product management capabilities:

• Utilising project management methodologies such as Agile, Scrum, or Lean to ensure efficient product development (Cervone, 2019).
- Gain a thorough understanding of various project management methodologies and their application in different contexts.
- Choose the most appropriate methodology based on the product's goals, team composition, and organisational culture.
- Implement the selected methodology consistently, ensuring the entire team understands and adheres to its principles and practices.

- Continuously evaluate the effectiveness of the chosen methodology and adapt it as needed to optimise product development processes.
- Focusing on strategic planning and prioritisation to allocate resources effectively (Ibarra & Scoular, 2019).
    - Conduct regular strategic planning sessions to identify the product's objectives, align them with organisational goals, and determine necessary resources.
    - Establish clear priorities and make informed decisions based on factors such as market demand, available resources, and potential return on investment.
    - Communicate priorities and expectations clearly to the team, ensuring that all members understand their roles and responsibilities.
    - Monitor progress and adjust priorities as needed to respond to changing circumstances or emerging opportunities.
- Developing risk management and quality assurance skills to mitigate potential issues and ensure product success (Kerzner, 2017).
    - Implement a systematic risk management process that involves identifying, analysing, and prioritising potential risks associated with product development.
    - Develop contingency plans and mitigation strategies to address identified risks and minimise their impact on the project.
    - Foster a culture of quality assurance by setting high standards for product performance, reliability, and user experience.
    - Implement regular testing and review processes to identify and address potential quality issues early in the development cycle.
- Enhance stakeholder management and communication skills (Müller, 2017).
    - Identify key stakeholders, including team members, customers, and upper management, and understand their needs, expectations, and concerns.

- Establish regular communication channels to keep stakeholders informed about project progress, challenges, and successes.
- Develop the ability to manage stakeholders' expectations by negotiating priorities, setting realistic deadlines, and managing scope changes.
- Utilise feedback from stakeholders to improve product development processes and outcomes.

By adopting these expanded strategies, technicians can effectively manage the development and execution of products, ensuring their success and aligning with organisational objectives.

Managing Customers

Technicians-turned-managers must also learn to manage customer relationships effectively. The following expanded strategies can help them achieve this goal:

- Developing communication skills to convey technical concepts to non-technical stakeholders (Reh, 2020).
    - Refine the ability to simplify complex technical concepts and present them in an accessible manner to non-technical audiences.
    - Utilise visual aids, analogies, and storytelling to make the technical information more engaging and easier to understand.
    - Practice active listening to ensure a clear understanding of customer needs, concerns, and expectations.
    - Enhance presentation skills to effectively communicate product features, benefits, and value propositions to customers.
- Fostering a customer-centric mindset within the team to ensure alignment with customer needs and expectations (Meyer & Schwager, 2007).
    - Emphasise the importance of understanding customer needs and preferences throughout the product development process.
    - Encourage team members to put themselves in the customers' shoes and consider their perspectives when making decisions.

- Establish processes to gather and analyse customer feedback regularly, ensuring that the team is responsive to customer needs and preferences.
- Celebrate and reward team members who demonstrate a strong focus on customer satisfaction and success.

• Utilising customer feedback and data to inform product development and improvement (Eichner, 2018).
- Implement a systematic approach to collecting customer feedback through various channels, such as surveys, interviews, and social media.
- Analyse customer feedback and data to identify trends, patterns, and areas for improvement.
- Incorporate customer insights into product development decisions, ensuring that products are tailored to meet customer needs and preferences.
- Regularly review and update product features and functionalities based on customer feedback, ensuring continuous improvement and adaptation to changing customer requirements.

• Building and maintaining long-term customer relationships (Levitt, 1983).
- Develop a proactive approach to customer relationship management by anticipating customer needs, addressing concerns, and offering solutions.
- Foster trust and credibility with customers by demonstrating a genuine interest in their success and consistently delivering on promises.
- Implement strategies to maintain regular contact with customers, such as newsletters, follow-up emails, and personal check-ins.
- Continuously seek opportunities to add value to customer relationships, such as providing relevant industry insights, sharing best practices, or offering additional support.

By employing these expanded strategies, technicians-turned-managers can effectively manage customer relationships, ensuring customer satisfaction and fostering long-term loyalty.

15. The Reluctant Leader

Retaining Core Skills, Enthusiasm, and Passion

To maintain enthusiasm and passion for their work, technicians transitioning to management roles should consider the following expanded strategies:

- Engage in continued professional development to stay current with industry trends and maintain technical expertise (HBR, 2021).
  - Participate in workshops, conferences, and online courses to stay informed about the latest advancements and best practices in their field.
  - Subscribe to industry publications, podcasts, and blogs to keep abreast of new developments and trends.
  - Pursue relevant certifications or advanced degrees to demonstrate commitment to professional growth and enhance credibility as a leader.
  - Foster a culture of continuous learning within the team by sharing knowledge, resources, and opportunities for professional development.
- Allocate time for hands-on technical work to maintain a connection to their core skills and interests (Kahnweiler, 2018).
  - Schedule regular blocks of time dedicated to hands-on technical tasks, such as troubleshooting, coding, or designing.
  - Identify opportunities to collaborate with team members on technical projects or provide expert guidance and support.
  - Seek out projects or initiatives within the organisation that align with personal technical interests and passions.
  - Balance management responsibilities with technical work to ensure a well-rounded approach that nurtures both leadership and technical skills.
- Cultivate a growth mindset to embrace new challenges and opportunities for learning (Dweck, 2006).
  - Develop a mindset that views challenges and setbacks as opportunities for growth rather than as failures or limitations.

- Encourage curiosity and a willingness to learn from mistakes, both personally and within the team.
- Set personal and professional goals that stretch capabilities and provide opportunities for learning and development.
- Foster a supportive environment where team members feel empowered to take risks, experiment, and learn from their experiences.
- Build a strong support network (Baldoni, 2005).
  - Establish relationships with mentors, peers, and other leaders who can provide guidance, support, and insights.
  - Participate in professional networks or industry associations to connect with like-minded individuals and exchange ideas and best practices.
  - Seek opportunities to collaborate with colleagues from diverse backgrounds and disciplines to gain fresh perspectives and broaden horizons.
  - Utilise the support network to share challenges, successes, and lessons learned, fostering a sense of camaraderie and shared growth.

By implementing these expanded strategies, technicians transitioning to management roles can maintain their enthusiasm and passion for their work while successfully adapting to the new challenges and responsibilities that come with leadership.

The Consequences of Unprepared Management

Promoting technicians to management roles without adequate training, support, or consideration for their willingness to lead can result in several negative consequences for both the individual and the organisation:

- Increased stress and burnout due to the added responsibilities and unfamiliarity with the role (Maslach et al., 2001).
  - Technicians may feel overwhelmed by the new expectations and challenges associated with their management position, leading to increased stress levels.

- The pressure to perform in a role that they may not have been adequately prepared for can contribute to burnout, negatively affecting their mental and physical health.
- Increased stress and burnout may also result in diminished job satisfaction, ultimately impacting overall performance and commitment to the organisation.

- Lower team morale and productivity resulting from ineffective leadership and poor communication (Eisenbeiss et al., 2013).
  - Without proper training and support, technicians may struggle to adapt their leadership style, communication, and problem-solving skills, leading to frustration and confusion among team members.
  - Poorly managed teams may experience reduced morale, lower productivity, and increased conflict, ultimately impacting the organisation's bottom line.
  - Ineffective leadership can also contribute to a toxic work environment, where team members feel unsupported, undervalued, or disengaged.
- A higher likelihood of the manager returning to an individual contributor role, resulting in turnover and instability within the organisation (Benson, 2021).
  - Technicians who feel ill-equipped to handle the responsibilities of a management role may choose to return to their previous technical roles or seek opportunities elsewhere.
  - High turnover rates can lead to organisational instability, increased recruitment and training costs, and the loss of valuable knowledge and skills.
  - The departure of a manager may also negatively impact team dynamics and trust, further exacerbating issues with morale and productivity.
- Hindered organisational growth and innovation (Charan, 2005).
  - Promoting unprepared technicians to management positions may result in a lack of strategic vision and direction, hindering the organisation's ability to adapt and grow in a competitive market.

- An ineffective manager may struggle to foster a culture of innovation and collaboration, limiting the organisation's capacity to develop new products, services, or solutions.
- Over time, these issues may contribute to a stagnation in organisational performance and an inability to keep pace with industry trends and developments.

By recognising and addressing these potential consequences, organisations can better support technicians transitioning to management roles, fostering success for both the individual and the organisation as a whole.

Organisational Recommendations

To support the successful transition of technicians to management roles, organisations should implement the following expanded strategies:

- Provide comprehensive leadership training programs that address skills such as emotional intelligence, delegation, and strategic planning (Kahnweiler, 2018).
    - Design and deliver customised training programs that cater to the unique challenges and responsibilities faced by technicians transitioning to management roles.
    - Incorporate real-world scenarios and case studies into training materials to ensure the practical application of newly learned skills and concepts.
    - Regularly assess and update training content to ensure its relevance and effectiveness in the ever-evolving business landscape.
    - Provide opportunities for technicians to practice their new skills in a safe and supportive environment, such as role-playing exercises or peer-feedback sessions.
- Offer mentorship opportunities with experienced managers to facilitate the sharing of knowledge and best practices (Bungay Stanier, 2016).
    - Pair technicians with seasoned managers who can provide guidance, advice, and support throughout the transition process.
    - Encourage open and honest communication between mentors and mentees, fostering an environment of trust and mutual learning.

- Facilitate regular check-ins and progress updates between mentors and mentees to monitor the development of new skills and address any challenges or concerns.
- Encourage mentors to share their own experiences, insights, and lessons learned, providing valuable context and inspiration for technicians navigating their new roles.

• Encourage a culture of continuous learning and professional development to support the growth of both individual contributors and managers (HBR, 2021).
  - Recognise and reward employees who demonstrate a commitment to ongoing learning and professional growth.
  - Provide resources and opportunities for employees to expand their knowledge and skills, such as access to online courses, industry conferences, or workshops.
  - Foster a collaborative environment where employees feel comfortable sharing their knowledge and expertise with one another, promoting collective growth and innovation.
  - Establish clear expectations around professional development and growth, encouraging employees to take ownership of their career trajectories and seek out opportunities for advancement.

• Monitor and evaluate the performance of technicians-turned-managers (Goleman, 2000).
  - Implement regular performance evaluations to assess the effectiveness of new managers and identify areas for improvement.
  - Provide constructive feedback and guidance to help technicians refine their management skills and address any performance gaps.
  - Celebrate and recognise the successes and achievements of new managers, reinforcing their confidence and commitment to their new roles.
  - Use performance evaluations as an opportunity to identify and address any ongoing challenges or barriers to success, ensuring that technicians have the necessary support and resources to excel in their management roles.

By employing these expanded strategies, organisations can effectively support the transition of technicians to management roles, fostering successful leadership development and promoting long-term organisational success.

Solving the Challenges

When technicians transition to management roles, they must navigate several challenges associated with managing people. This section further expands on these challenges and provides practical adaptation strategies for technicians to become effective managers.

So, what are some of the challenges and how might the new manager adapt their skills to support the changes?

Challenge: Building Trust and Rapport

Technicians may struggle to build trust and rapport with their team members, which is crucial for successful leadership (Northouse, 2018).

Adaptation Strategy: To build trust and rapport, technicians should focus on open communication, active listening, and demonstrating genuine concern for their team members. By sharing information transparently, acknowledging team members' opinions, and being responsive to their needs, technicians can foster a supportive and inclusive environment (Edmondson, 2019).

Challenge: Balancing Technical and Managerial Work

Technicians may find it difficult to strike a balance between their technical work and managerial responsibilities (Benson, 2021).

Adaptation Strategy: Time management is crucial in balancing these responsibilities. Technicians should prioritise tasks, set boundaries, and allocate dedicated time for both managerial and technical work (Morgenstern, 2004). This will help ensure that they can continue to contribute technically while effectively managing their team

Challenge: Resolving Conflict

Conflict resolution is an essential skill for managers but may be unfamiliar territory for technicians (Runde & Flanagan, 2010)

Adaptation Strategy: To navigate conflicts effectively, technicians should develop their negotiation and problem-solving skills. Emphasising open communication, empathising with different perspectives, and seeking mutually beneficial solutions can help diffuse tensions and promote a collaborative work environment (Fisher & Ury, 2011).

Challenge: Motivating and Engaging Team Members

Keeping team members motivated and engaged is critical for productivity and job satisfaction but may be challenging for new managers (Pink, 2011).

Adaptation Strategy: Technicians should strive to understand their team members' intrinsic and extrinsic motivators and tailor their management approach accordingly. By providing autonomy, offering opportunities for growth, and recognising achievements, technicians can boost motivation and engagement levels within their team (Pink, 2011).

Challenge: Navigating Organisational Politics

Technicians may be unprepared to deal with the complexities of organisational politics that often accompany management roles (Pfeffer, 2010).

Adaptation Strategy: To successfully navigate organisational politics, technicians should develop strong networking skills, cultivate alliances, and stay informed about organisational changes and dynamics. By understanding the political landscape, technicians can make informed decisions and strategically position themselves and their teams for success (Pfeffer, 2010).

Conclusion

The successful adaptation of technical skills to management roles is essential for individual contributors and technicians transitioning to leadership positions. By focusing on the development of essential management skills, such as emotional intelligence, delegation, strategic planning, and communication, while retaining core technical expertise, enthusiasm, and passion, these reluctant leaders can become effective managers.

Organisations play a crucial role in supporting this transition and should invest in comprehensive training programs, mentorship opportunities, and a culture of continuous learning and professional development. This not only facilitates the growth of technicians turned-managers but also contributes to the overall success and resilience of the organisation.

Additionally, organisations must recognise the potential negative consequences of placing unprepared individuals in management roles, such as increased stress and burnout, lower team morale and productivity, and higher turnover rates. By proactively addressing these issues through targeted interventions and support systems, organisations can mitigate risks and help technicians successfully navigate the challenges of their new leadership roles.

The key to a successful transition from a technician to a manager lies in striking a balance between honing essential management skills and maintaining a connection to one's technical expertise and passion. Organisations that prioritise the development and support of technicians as they step into leadership positions will not only foster individual success but also promote a thriving and innovative work environment that benefits the entire organisation.

Good Luck in your new role if you are a new or aspiring manager!

References & Further Reading

Baldoni, J. (2005). Great Communication Secrets of Great Leaders. New York: McGrawHill.

Benson, R. (2021). The Accidental Manager: The Rise of the Reluctant Leader. London: Kogan Page.

Bungay Stanier, M. (2016). The Coaching Habit: Say Less, Ask More & Change the Way You Lead Forever. Toronto: Box of Crayons Press.

Catalyst. (2020). Building Inclusive Workplaces. Retrieved from https://www.catalyst.org/research/building-inclusive-workplaces/

Cervone, H. F. (2019). An overview of Agile project management. OCLC Systems & Services: International Digital Library Perspectives, 35(1), 2-5.

Charan, R. (2005). Ending the CEO Succession Crisis. Harvard Business Review. Retrieved from https://hbr.org/2005/02/ending-the-ceo-succession-crisis

Dweck, C. S. (2006). Mindset: The New Psychology of Success. New York: Random House.

Edmondson, A. (2019). The Fearless Organization: Creating Psychological Safety in the Workplace for Learning, Innovation, and Growth. Hoboken, NJ: Wiley.

Eichner, J. (2018). The Power of Customer Feedback. Harvard Business Review. Retrieved from https://hbr.org/2018/10/the-power-of-customer-feedback

Eichner, J. (2018). The Customer-Driven Playbook: Converting Customer Feedback into Successful Products. Sebastopol, CA: O'Reilly Media.

Eisenbeiss, S. A., Knippenberg, D. V., & Boerner, S. (2013). Age and leadership: The moderating role of legacy beliefs. The Leadership Quarterly, 24(5), 725-744.

Fisher, R., & Ury, W. (2011). Getting to Yes: Negotiating Agreement Without Giving In. New York: Penguin Books.

15. The Reluctant Leader

Goleman, D. (2004). *What Makes a Leader?* Harvard Business Review. Retrieved from https://hbr.org/2004/01/what-makes-a-leader

Goleman, D. (2000). *Leadership That Gets Results.* Harvard Business Review. Retrieved from https://hbr.org/2000/03/leadership-that-gets-results

Harvard Business Review (HBR). (2021). *The Key to Continued Professional Growth.* Retrieved from https://hbr.org/2021/08/the-key-to-continued-professional-growth

HBR. (2021). *How to Keep Learning and Still Have a Life.* Harvard Business Review. Retrieved from https://hbr.org/2021/09/how-to-keep-learning-and-still-have-a-life

Ibarra, H., & Scoular, A. (2019). *The Leader as Coach.* Harvard Business Review. Retrieved from https://hbr.org/2019/11/the-leader-as-coach

Kahnweiler, J. B. (2018). *The Introverted Leader: Building on Your Quiet Strength.* Oakland, CA: Berrett-Koehler Publishers.

Kerzner, H. (2017). *Project Management: A Systems Approach to Planning, Scheduling, and Controlling.* Hoboken, NJ: Wiley.

Levitt, T. (1983). *After the Sale is Over.* Harvard Business Review. Retrieved from https://hbr.org/1983/09/after-the-sale-is-over

Maslach, C., Schaufeli, W. B., & Leiter, M. P. (2001). *Job burnout.* Annual Review of Psychology, 52, 397-422.

Meyer, C., & Schwager, A. (2007). *Understanding Customer Experience.* Harvard Business Review. Retrieved from https://hbr.org/2007/02/understanding-customer-experience

Morgenstern, J. (2004). *Time Management from the Inside Out: The Foolproof System for Taking Control of Your Schedule and Your Life.* New York: Henry Holt and Company.

Müller, R. (2017). *Project Management Communication Tools.* Plantation, FL: J. Ross Publishing.

Northouse, P. G. (2018). *Leadership: Theory and Practice.* Thousand Oaks, CA: SAGE Publications.

Pfeffer, J. (2010). *Power: Why Some People Have It and Others Don't.* New York: HarperBusiness.

Pink, D. H. (2011). *Drive: The Surprising Truth About What Motivates Us.* New York: Riverhead Books.

Reh, F. J. (2020). *Improve Your Communication Skills in Just One Day.* The Balance Careers. Retrieved from https://www.thebalancecareers.com/improve-your-communicationskills-2276096

Runde, C. E., & Flanagan, T. A. (2010). *Becoming a Conflict Competent Leader: How You and Your Organization Can Manage Conflict Effectively.* San Francisco, CA: Jossey-Bass.

Rachael Evans MA, FCMI

16. The Toxic Employee Dilemma

Last week's coaching theme was an interesting one. One of my mentees, a business owner, is struggling with a long-term toxic employee. We discussed how they would validate if the individual was demotivated or was genuinely toxic, what the toxicity types are, and if their analysis highlighted that the individual was indeed a toxic employee, what steps they can, and should take.

This is, unfortunately, one of the toughest challenges you may face as a business leader, navigating the murky waters of workplace conflict, particularly when dealing with a toxic employee. I know I have never been comfortable when dealing with such issues as it can feel personal when faced with the individuals behaviour.

Often, we look outside for guidance, to others, and increasingly so, to sources such as LinkedIn. Whilst resources like LinkedIn offer numerous insights, it's essential to discern helpful guidance from misleading, inexperienced, agenda-tilted, or simply superficial advice. There's a lot of it on LinkedIn from inexperienced managers right now and it made sense to summarise this in a short article.

What Does a Toxic Employee Look Like?

A toxic employee isn't just someone who occasionally has a bad day. This individual consistently exhibits behaviours detrimental to team morale and productivity. Their actions can undermine projects, drain emotional energy, and even drive talented employees away.

Here are some attributes of toxic employees:

- **Persistent Negativity**: They constantly complain, spread rumours, or are always pessimistic.
- **Manipulative Behaviour**: They may use information against others, gossip, or pit colleagues against each other.
- **Reluctance to Admit Mistakes:** They always play the blame game, refusing to take responsibility.
- **Bullying or Intimidation**: They use their position, or sometimes just sheer aggression, to intimidate others.

Identifying a Toxic Employee

- **Listen to Team Feedback**: Your team often feels the impact first. If multiple employees voice concerns about a colleague, it's a sign to investigate further.
- **Consistent Patterns**: While everyone can have an off day, toxic behaviours are repetitive and form patterns over time.
- **Decline in Team Morale or Productivity**: If you notice a sudden change in team dynamics or productivity after a particular employee joins, it's worth taking a closer look.

Types of Toxicity

Toxic behaviours can manifest in various ways, and it's crucial to identify the kind of toxicity you're dealing with. Does the individual fall into one or more of these four categories?

1. **The Gossip**: Thrives on rumours, often spreading or exaggerating information.
2. **The Victim**: Constantly feels they are being targeted, even when provided with constructive feedback.

3. **The Slacker**: Avoids tasks, pushes responsibilities onto others, and lacks accountability.
4. **The Aggressor**: Uses aggressive behaviour or language, making colleagues feel uncomfortable or threatened.

Addressing the Issue: What Can You Do?

- **Open Dialogue**: Initiate a one-on-one discussion. Address your concerns and provide specific examples. Allow the employee to voice their perspective.
- **Documentation**: Keep a record of instances of toxic behaviour. This documentation can clarify patterns and, if necessary, in taking disciplinary actions.
- **Offer Feedback and Coaching**: Some employees may not be aware of their toxic behaviour. Offering feedback, coupled with resources like coaching or training, can be beneficial.
- **Set Clear Boundaries**: Clearly communicate what behaviours are unacceptable and what consequences will ensue if they continue.
- **Know When to Take Direct Action**: Sometimes, after all efforts, the best solution may be to part ways with the toxic employee. Keeping a damaging influence can be more harmful in the long run.

While platforms like LinkedIn can offer helpful insights, it's crucial to approach advice critically and recognise when direct action is needed. Every organisation deserves a healthy work environment. As a leader/ manager, taking decisive steps against toxicity not only benefits your team but the entire company's culture and productivity. Remember, addressing toxicity isn't just about removing a problem but fostering an environment where everyone can thrive.

Rachael Evans MA, FCMI

17. Voluntary Participation in Management Coaching – Don't Force it!

You've only got to look at the content on LinkedIn to realise that management coaching has become a ubiquitous tool for leadership development, productivity enhancement, and overall workplace improvement. Yet, the way this tool is deployed can dramatically impact its effectiveness. I'd like to shed light on why management coaching should be a voluntary process, initiated by the individual who wishes to be coached, rather than being enforced from above by management to address a perceived issue.

Let's start with a look at the problems behind implementing a forced-coaching engagement model as for many, this is their initial experience of coaching. It's either suggested by management or, perhaps you are thinking of suggesting it yourself.

The Problem with Enforced Coaching

In any developmental programme, the way it is implemented can be as crucial as the content itself. When coaching becomes a mandatory exercise, rather than a voluntary choice, a host of complications can arise. These challenges not only affect the individual involved but can also have ripple effects throughout an organisation. So, what are those challenges?

Lack of Intrinsic Motivation

One of the cornerstones of any successful coaching relationship is intrinsic motivation—the deep-rooted desire to evolve and improve. When coaching is mandated by an external authority, the individual being coached often lacks this intrinsic drive. Consequently, their engagement levels plummet, severely compromising the effectiveness of the coaching programme.

Resistance and Resentment

Enforced coaching can elicit strong feelings of resistance and resentment among employees. The implication that one needs coaching can be perceived as an indictment of their capabilities, which may have detrimental effects on an employee's self-esteem and, by extension, workplace morale.

Wasted Resources

Enforced coaching is a resource-intensive exercise that may not yield commensurate returns. Not only are financial investments involved in terms of the coach's fees, but there is also the expenditure of time for both parties. These resources could be more fruitfully applied to individuals who are intrinsically motivated to improve.

Counterproductive Outcomes

When coaching is enforced, the likelihood of counterproductive outcomes increases. The coachee may become demotivated, further distancing themselves from organisational objectives. This kind of disengagement can lead to a decline in productivity, negatively affecting the entire team and potentially contaminating the workplace culture. The picture however is far from negative, especially when the coachee has either requested or indeed has sought out coaching. There are untold benefits behind voluntary or self-selected coaching

The Benefits of Voluntary Coaching

When it comes to personal and professional development, the approach taken can significantly influence the outcomes. Opting into a coaching programme voluntarily brings with it a variety of advantages that go beyond the individual and can positively impact the wider organisation. Let's explore the multifaceted benefits of choosing to engage in coaching of one's own accord.

Self-Initiative

Individuals who proactively seek out coaching are more likely to be vested in their personal and professional growth. This intrinsic motivation not only leads to higher levels of commitment but also increases the likelihood of sustained behavioural change, making the coaching far more effective.

Customised, Goal-Oriented Coaching

When coaching is sought voluntarily, it is often easier for the coach to tailor their approach to the specific needs and objectives of the coachee. This customisation enhances the effectiveness of the coaching, making it more goal oriented and result-driven.

Enhanced Workplace

Culture In an environment where coaching is voluntary, the overall workplace culture stands to benefit. Employees feel empowered and valued, knowing that they have the autonomy to seek out developmental resources. This atmosphere promotes a continuous learning mentality, encouraging everyone to strive for excellence.

Efficient Utilisation of Resources

From a business perspective, voluntary coaching often ensures a higher return on investment (ROI). Because the coaching is more targeted and the participants more committed, the likelihood of achieving the desired outcomes increases, thereby justifying the expenditure of time and resources.

In Closing

Management coaching can be an incredibly effective tool for personal and organisational growth. However, the way it is implemented can significantly affect its success. For optimal outcomes, coaching should be a voluntary process, ideally driven by individuals who are motivated to improve. Mandating coaching not only risks diminishing its effectiveness but can also have a host of negative ramifications, from wasted resources to diminished employee morale. By fostering an organisational culture that encourages voluntary coaching, companies pave the way for more meaningful development, higher levels of employee engagement, and ultimately, a more harmonious and productive work environment.

Krysten M. Bacan

18. The Double-Edged Sword: The 'Cult of Personality' and its Implications for Expanding Businesses

The phenomenon of the 'cult of personality' in business leadership is a subject that has garnered both admiration and scrutiny. While charismatic leaders often drive innovation, mobilise workforces, and catalyse growth, the repercussions of such concentrated influence in expanding businesses are less discussed. This article provides a comprehensive exploration of the merits and drawbacks of the 'cult of personality' as it applies to growing businesses. Utilising academic references and theoretical frameworks, the article systematically examines key dimensions such as inspirational leadership, rapid decision-making, employee engagement, leadership bottlenecks, employee turnover, and institutional deficiencies. A case study of the healthcare company Theranos illustrates the practical implications of charismatic leadership gone awry. The article concludes with recommendations for balancing the potential benefits and inherent risks of such leadership styles in the context of business expansion.

Introduction

In the annals of business history, charismatic figures such as Steve Jobs, Elon Musk and Richard Branson are often hailed as visionary leaders who have revolutionised industries. Their larger-than-life personas capture imaginations, sway investors, and galvanise employees. Such figures epitomise the concept of the 'cult of personality,' where an individual's charisma, vision, and leadership style become deeply entwined with the organisation's identity and success. However, beneath the surface gloss lies a complex and often problematic dynamic that can pose significant challenges, particularly for businesses in expansionary phases.

Objectives and Scope

This article aims to dissect the phenomenon of the 'cult of personality' in growing businesses, examining both its merits and drawbacks. Through academic references, theoretical frameworks, and a detailed case study of Theranos—once a rising star in the healthcare sector—this article explores the dimensions of inspirational leadership, quick decision-making, employee engagement, and leadership bottlenecks. It also delves into issues such as high employee turnover and the lack of institutionalisation, which can become particularly acute as companies scale up.

Why This Matters

The topic is especially relevant in today's fast-paced, competitive business environment, where charismatic leadership is often considered a unique selling proposition (USP) for start-ups and small enterprises looking to scale. Understanding the complexities involved can provide valuable insights for stakeholders ranging from entrepreneurs and investors to policymakers and scholars.

Roadmap

Following this introduction, the article will explore various aspects of the 'cult of personality' through theoretical discussions and a comprehensive case study. It will culminate in a conclusion that synthesizes key learnings and offers recommendations for how growing businesses can navigate the challenges and opportunities that come with a charismatic leader at the helm.

The Charismatic Pull: Strengths

Inspirational Leadership

Inspirational leadership is often cited as one of the most compelling advantages of a 'cult of personality' within a growing business. The power of a charismatic leader to inspire an organisation cannot be overstated.

Visionary Thinking

Leaders with a 'cult of personality' often possess an uncanny ability to see beyond the horizon, forecasting opportunities and challenges that others fail to perceive. Steve Jobs, for example, envisioned a world where personal computing would revolutionise the way people interact, long before the idea became mainstream. His vision for the iPhone as an extension of oneself radically shifted the paradigm of mobile communication (Isaacson, 2011).

Cultivating a Shared Identity

Charismatic leaders effectively cultivate a sense of shared identity and purpose among employees. Mark Zuckerberg's early motto for Facebook, "Move fast and break things," served not just as a strategic directive but also as a rallying cry that encapsulated the company's ethos (Kirkpatrick, 2010).

Mobilising Resources

Inspirational leaders are adept at mobilising both human and financial resources. Oprah Winfrey's transition from a talk-show host to a media mogul exemplifies the ability to motivate a team while also securing significant investments. Her OWN network, although initially struggling, succeeded due to her ability to attract both talent and capital (Garofalo, 2019).

Emotional Resonance

An often overlooked yet crucial aspect of inspirational leadership is the emotional resonance a charismatic leader can create. Leaders such as Nelson Mandela and Mahatma Gandhi were not just strategic thinkers but also emotionally intelligent individuals who could empathise, inspire, and mobilise mass support (Goleman, 1995).

The Feedback Loop

A charismatic leader's inspiration feeds back into the organisation, creating a virtuous circle. Employees who are highly motivated tend to be more productive, which in turn enhances the company's performance and solidifies the leader's standing, thereby perpetuating the cycle of inspiration (Avolio et al., 2004).

Potential Pitfalls

However, the focus on inspirational leadership should not obfuscate the risks. Inspiration can easily tip over into idealisation, where the leader's vision becomes a blinding force, making it difficult for employees to critically assess potential flaws or setbacks. There also remains the risk of perpetuating a dependency culture within the organisation, as employees may defer excessively to the charismatic figure at the helm (Conger & Kanungo, 1998).

Quick Decision Making

Quick decision-making is often lauded as one of the distinct advantages of having a charismatic leader at the helm of an organisation. The ability to make rapid, decisive judgments is especially vital in an era marked by volatility, uncertainty, complexity, and ambiguity—commonly referred to as the 'VUCA' world.

Responsiveness to Market Changes

Leaders who possess a cult of personality tend to have an intuitive understanding of market trends, giving them an edge in making swift decisions that capitalize on opportunities. For instance, Reed Hastings' decision to split Netflix's DVD rental service from its streaming business was met with public backlash initially but proved to be a visionary move in hindsight (Keating, 2012).

Crisis Management

During times of crisis, quick decision-making is not just an asset—it's a necessity. One could consider the actions of Howard Schultz, who, upon returning as CEO of Starbucks in 2008, immediately took radical steps like shutting down all US stores for retraining and discontinuing poorly performing products. These quick decisions played a significant role in Starbucks' turnaround (Schultz & Yang, 2011).

Autonomy and Efficiency

Charismatic leaders often bypass bureaucratic processes, thereby streamlining operations. Elon Musk's announcement on Twitter to consider taking Tesla private—an unorthodox and lightning-fast corporate disclosure—is one extreme example of how quick decision-making can be executed (Vance, 2015).

Leveraging Emotional Intelligence

Quick decisions by charismatic leaders often tap into the collective emotional pulse of the organisation and its stakeholders. The decisions are thus not only cognitive but also emotive in nature, thereby resonating at multiple levels within the organisation (Goleman, 1998).

18. The Cult of Personality

The Dark Side of Quick Decision Making

Despite these advantages, swift decision-making carries inherent risks. Quick choices can lead to errors that are not easily reversible and can have long-term repercussions. For example, Travis Kalanick's quick decision to launch Uber in China without fully understanding the market dynamics led to a costly exit later (Lashinsky, 2017).

Moreover, a culture that values speed over deliberation may discourage dissent and critical evaluation, leading to groupthink (Janis, 1972). Quick decisions could also create stress and frustration among employees who feel side-lined in the decision-making process (Bass & Riggio, 2006).

Employee Engagement

One of the most palpable benefits of a 'cult of personality' in a business setting is the heightened level of employee engagement that often accompanies charismatic leadership.

Elevation of Morale

A charismatic leader often serves as a source of inspiration that galvanises the workforce. For example, Sheryl Sandberg's concept of "leaning in" has inspired countless women at Facebook and beyond to engage more actively in their careers (Sandberg, 2013).

Fostering a Sense of Belonging

Leaders with a strong personality often create an organisational culture where employees feel like they are a part of something larger than themselves. Howard Schultz, for example, stressed that Starbucks partners (employees) are part of a mission to inspire and nurture the human spirit (Schultz & Yang, 2011).

Personalised Communication

Effective leaders leverage their charisma to establish direct, personal connections with employees. Richard Branson's open and approachable leadership style is often cited as a key factor behind Virgin's high employee engagement levels (Branson, 2012).

Intellectual Stimulation

Charismatic leaders often engage their employees on an intellectual level, challenging them to think creatively and solve problems. This not only increases job satisfaction but also enhances productivity. Google's Sundar Pichai, for example, encourages open dialogue and innovative thinking, which has been linked to higher employee engagement (Bock, 2015).

Trust and Loyalty

In organisations where a charismatic leader is at the helm, employees often develop a deep sense of trust and loyalty towards the leader. This level of engagement is closely correlated with lower turnover and higher job satisfaction (Mayer et al., 1995).

The Pitfalls of Over-Engagement

While the above aspects paint a largely positive picture, over-reliance on a charismatic leader for employee engagement can have downsides. Over-engagement can lead to burnout, and loyalty towards a leader should not be conflated with loyalty towards the organisation (Maslach & Leiter, 1997). In extreme cases, excessive engagement can even facilitate a toxic work culture, where the leader's flaws are overlooked or excused, leading to ethical lapses (Kellerman, 2004).

A Tightrope Walk: Challenges

Leadership Bottlenecks

While charismatic leadership offers many advantages, including inspirational vision and increased employee engagement, it also often introduces the challenge of leadership bottlenecks. These are points where the decision-making process or the operational flow of the business gets constrained due to the overriding influence or control of a single leader.

Centralised Decision-Making

Charismatic leaders often have a strong preference for making key decisions themselves. While this centralisation can lead to quick and cohesive decision-making, it also presents a significant bottleneck, especially in larger, more complex organisations. For example, the late Steve Jobs at Apple was notorious for having the final say on a wide range of issues, from product design to marketing strategies (Isaacson, 2011).

Diminished Middle Management

In a cult of personality, middle managers can find their roles diminished, as employees may bypass them to seek approval directly from the top. This dynamic was evident at Tesla under Elon Musk, where the CEO's active involvement in multiple layers of the organisation led to challenges in scaling operations efficiently (Vance, 2015).

Innovation Stagnation

Although charismatic leaders are often heralded as innovators, their very presence can stifle the creativity of other employees who might hesitate to propose alternative ideas. Jeff Bezos's role at Amazon has been questioned on similar grounds, given his enormous influence over the company's strategic direction (Stone, 2013).

Resource Allocation

The focus of both human and financial resources often gravitates towards projects directly under the charismatic leader's purview. This can result in inefficient resource allocation and hamper the growth of other valuable projects within the company (Kellerman, 2004).

The 'Single Point of Failure' Risk

In extreme cases, the entire organisation may become so dependent on its charismatic leader that any harm to or departure of this individual poses an existential threat to the organisation. A case in point would be the uncertainty surrounding Berkshire Hathaway's future after Warren Buffett (Cunningham, 2014).

Ethical Quandaries

Charismatic leaders can sometimes exploit their influence to bypass checks and balances, leading to questionable decisions. Elizabeth Holmes of Theranos provides a cautionary tale of how leadership bottlenecks can contribute to corporate misconduct (Carreyrou, 2018).

Employee Turnover

While charismatic leaders can inspire and motivate their workforce to new heights, this same magnetism can contribute to fluctuating levels of employee turnover, both positively and negatively.

Decreased Turnover through Loyalty and Engagement

Leaders with strong personalities and a sense of mission often create work environments where employees are deeply engaged and committed to the company's goals. Richard Branson's Virgin Group, for example, boasts notably low employee turnover rates, attributed to Branson's unique brand of charismatic leadership (Branson, 2012).

Attraction and Retention of Talent

A charismatic leader can serve as a magnet for talent. Many highly skilled individuals are attracted to work under visionary leaders like Elon Musk, seeking to be part of ground-breaking projects like SpaceX's Mars missions (Vance, 2015).

Turnover Due to Burnout and Stress

On the other side of the coin, the demanding environment fostered by some charismatic leaders can lead to employee burnout and consequently higher turnover. The intensity of working for Steve Jobs at Apple was well-documented, with many employees finding the environment too challenging for long-term commitment (Isaacson, 2011).

Turnover Due to a 'Cult of Personality'

In extreme cases, the very essence of a 'cult of personality' can lead to significant employee turnover. Those who are not fully aligned with the leader's vision or methods may find themselves feeling isolated or marginalized, prompting them to leave. Travis Kalanick's tenure at Uber exemplifies how a strong personality, for all its advantages, can also polarize the workforce, contributing to high employee turnover (Lashinsky, 2017).

Departure of the Charismatic Leader

Interestingly, the departure or absence of a charismatic leader can also lead to a significant spike in employee turnover. The aura they create often binds the team, and their departure can lead to a sense of disillusionment or disorientation among employees. This phenomenon was observed at Apple following the death of Steve Jobs, where several key executives and many employees left the company (Kane & Sherr, 2014).

Lack of Institutionalisation

One of the most overlooked challenges that a 'cult of personality' brings to a growing business is the lack of institutionalisation, which refers to the failure to embed key processes, values, and competencies within the organisation. Instead, these elements are often tethered to the charismatic leader, leading to a range of vulnerabilities.

Inconsistency in Leadership and Management

Charismatic leaders often prefer intuitive decision-making over established protocols. While this allows for agility and innovation, it also generates inconsistencies in leadership and management practices. For instance, the absence of standard operating procedures can make the business too dependent on the individual flair of the leader, as seen during the tenure of Carly Fiorina at Hewlett-Packard (Burrows & Grover, 2005).

Lack of Succession Planning

Given that much of the company's identity and strategy may be closely tied to the leader's personality, succession planning becomes especially challenging. This was evident in Apple's transition period following Steve Jobs' passing, where the company initially struggled to maintain its innovative edge (Kane & Sherr, 2014).

Limited Scalability

As businesses grow, the need for institutional structures becomes imperative for scalability. Lack of institutionalisation under a charismatic leader can hinder the company's ability to scale efficiently, as evidenced by Uber's challenges in professionalising its business operations post-Travis Kalanick (Lashinsky, 2017).

Knowledge Drain

The exit of a charismatic leader can result in a severe loss of institutional knowledge if robust systems and processes are not in place. This 'brain drain' can significantly affect the business's operations and continuity. Microsoft experienced such a challenge when Bill Gates stepped down, requiring significant reorganisation to fill the knowledge void (Rivkin & Siggelkow, 2002).

Vulnerability to Ethical Lapses

A lack of institutional checks and balances can result in the leader's personality becoming the de facto ethical compass for the organisation. Such an environment increases the risk of ethical lapses, exemplified by the scandals at Theranos under Elizabeth Holmes (Carreyrou, 2018).

Case Study: Theranos - The Perils of a 'Cult of Personality'

Founded in 2003 by Elizabeth Holmes, Theranos aimed to revolutionise the medical testing industry with its proprietary technology. Holmes' charismatic leadership was the centrifugal force behind the company's initial rapid growth, but as the business expanded, the same charismatic allure became a crippling weakness.

Inspirational Leadership Gone Awry

Holmes inspired her employees with a vision of changing the world through affordable, accessible healthcare testing (Carreyrou, 2018). However, this inspiration turned into an almost blind faith in Holmes' vision, overshadowing the scientific inaccuracies and impracticalities associated with Theranos' technology.

Quick Decision-Making But at What Cost?

Holmes' decisions were often swift but lacked validation, largely because she managed to create an environment where dissent was discouraged. This lack of peer review or oversight led to incorrect choices, such as misleading investors and partners about the technology's capabilities (Carreyrou, 2018).

Employee Turnover and Brain Drain

Many talented employees who questioned the validity of Theranos' technology eventually left, disillusioned by the toxic environment and blatant disregard for ethical considerations. The high turnover rate resulted in a loss of intellectual capital and increased the company's vulnerability (Carreyrou, 2018).

Lack of Institutionalisation

Holmes' dominant personality and centralized control meant that there were limited protocols and checks within the organization. The lack of institutionalised governance made it easier for Theranos to engage in corporate misconduct, including manipulating test results and lying to regulators (Carreyrou, 2018).

Leadership Bottlenecks and Ethical Lapses

Holmes' overwhelming influence also led to leadership bottlenecks, as most decisions had to go through her. Coupled with a lack of ethical oversight, this led to disastrous consequences, such as the roll-out of inaccurate blood tests to consumers (Carreyrou, 2018).

The Fall

When the shortcomings of Theranos were eventually exposed, the company fell from a $9 billion valuation to being worthless, leading to legal repercussions for Holmes and a loss of credibility for many who endorsed her (Carreyrou, 2018).

Conclusion:

The influence of charismatic leaders on growing businesses presents a compelling paradox. On one hand, such leaders often serve as the catalyst for innovation, employee engagement, and rapid growth. Their ability to articulate a compelling vision can attract high-calibre talent and foster a culture of loyalty and dedication. Companies led by such figures often stand out in competitive landscapes, garnering media attention and investor interest. Yet, as explored through academic insights and illustrated by the cautionary tale of Theranos, these strengths can quickly become liabilities if not carefully managed.

The Duality of Influence

Charismatic leadership, in essence, is a double-edged sword. While it can lead to rapid decision-making, employee engagement, and a unifying corporate culture, it can also result in leadership bottlenecks, high employee turnover, ethical lapses, and a dangerous lack of institutionalisation. The challenges become especially pronounced as businesses transition from start-up to scale-up phases, requiring a level of structural and procedural maturity that a 'cult of personality' often inhibits.

Future-proofing Leadership

As businesses grow, the need for embedding robust institutional practices becomes imperative. Leaders must work consciously to institutionalise processes, introduce checks and balances, and develop a culture of collective responsibility. It is in this context that the lessons of the Theranos case study become particularly poignant. Elizabeth Holmes' initially inspirational leadership devolved into a cautionary example of what can go wrong when an organization's fortunes are too tightly bound to a single, charismatic figure.

Final Thoughts

In closing, the allure of charismatic leadership in business is undeniable, but it comes with complex challenges that require nuanced handling. Growing businesses must strive to balance the inspiring vision of their leaders with the practical needs for governance, scalability, and sustainability. This calls for a proactive approach to management that acknowledges the benefits and drawbacks of having a dominant, charismatic leader. Future research and case studies may provide further insights into how this delicate balance can be best achieved, but the foundational principles are clear: foresight, adaptability, and a commitment to ethical and procedural rigour are crucial.

References

Avolio, B. J., Walumbwa, F. O., & Weber, T. J. (2004). Leadership: Current Theories, Research, and Future Directions. Annual Review of Psychology, 60, 421–449.

Bass, B. M., & Riggio, R. E. (2006). Transformational Leadership. Psychology Press.

Bock, L. (2015). Work Rules!: Insights from Inside Google That Will Transform How You Live and Lead. Hachette UK.

Branson, R. (2012). Like a Virgin: Secrets They Won't Teach You at Business School. Virgin Books.

Buffett, W., & Clark, D. (1999). Buffettology. Scribner.

Burrows, P., & Grover, R. (2005). Carly's Way. Business Week, 10, 34-40.

Carreyrou, J. (2018). Bad Blood: Secrets and Lies in a Silicon Valley Startup. Knopf.

Chen, Z., Lam, W., & Zhong, J. A. (2018). Leader-member exchange and employee turnover intentions: A social identity perspective. Journal of Organizational Behavior, 39(5), 645–658.

Collins, J. (2001). Good to Great: Why Some Companies Make the Leap... and Others Don't. HarperCollins.

Conger, J. A., & Kanungo, R. N. (1998). Charismatic Leadership in Organizations. Sage.

Cunningham, L. A. (2014). Berkshire Beyond Buffett: The Enduring Value of Values. Columbia University Press.

Drucker, P. (2001). The Essential Drucker. HarperBusiness.

Garofalo, D. (2019). Oprah Winfrey: A Biography. Greenhaven Press.

Goffee, R., & Jones, G. (2006). Why Should Anyone Be Led by You?. Harvard Business School Press.

Goleman, D. (1995). Emotional Intelligence. Bantam Books.

Goleman, D. (1998). Working with Emotional Intelligence. Bantam Books.

Isaacson, W. (2011). Steve Jobs. Simon & Schuster.

Janis, I. L. (1972). *Victims of Groupthink*. Houghton Mifflin.

Kane, Y. I., & Sherr, I. (2014). *Haunted Empire: Apple After Steve Jobs*. HarperCollins.

Keating, G. (2012). *Netflixed: The Epic Battle for America's Eyeballs*. Portfolio/Penguin.

Kellerman, B. (2004). *Bad Leadership: What It Is, How It Happens, Why It Matters*. Harvard Business Review Press.

Khurana, R. (2002). *Searching for a Corporate Savior: The Irrational Quest for Charismatic CEOs*. Princeton University Press.

Kirkpatrick, D. (2010). *The Facebook Effect*. Simon & Schuster.

Kouzes, J. M., & Posner, B. Z. (2017). *The Leadership Challenge: How to Make Extraordinary Things Happen in Organizations*. Wiley.

Lashinsky, A. (2017). *Wild Ride: Inside Uber's Quest for World Domination*. Portfolio/Penguin.

Maccoby, M. (2000). *Narcissistic Leaders: Who Succeeds and Who Fails*. Harvard Business School Press.

Maslach, C., & Leiter, M. P. (1997). *The Truth About Burnout: How Organizations Cause Personal Stress and What to Do About It*. Jossey-Bass.

Mayer, R. C., Davis, J. H., & Schoorman, F. D. (1995). An Integrative Model of Organizational Trust. *Academy of Management Review, 20*(3), 709-734.

Rivkin, J. W., & Siggelkow, N. (2002). Organizational Sticking Points on NK Landscapes. *Complexity, 7*(5), 31-43.

Sandberg, S. (2013). *Lean In: Women, Work, and the Will to Lead*. Knopf.

Sinek, S. (2009). *Start with Why: How Great Leaders Inspire Everyone to Take Action*. Portfolio.

Schultz, H., & Yang, D. J. (2011). *Pour Your Heart Into It: How Starbucks Built a Company One Cup at a Time*. Hyperion.

Stone, B. (2013). *The Everything Store: Jeff Bezos and the Age of Amazon*. Little, Brown.

Vance, A. (2015). *Elon Musk: Tesla, SpaceX, and the Quest for a Fantastic Future*. HarperCollins.

Wiedeman, R. (2020). *Billion Dollar Loser: The Epic Rise and Spectacular Fall of Adam Neumann and WeWork*. Little, Brown and Company.

About NewEdj

Founded in 2022 in the US and Europe, NewEdj was formed from the coming together of two business leaders, Krysten Bacan and Rachael Evans. Krysten, a 30-year veteran of MSP service management and Rachael, business strategy, transformation and Banking, bring a new type of advisory firm to it's clients.

Tired of seeing solutions designed by the big consultants who overpromised and underdelivered whilst treating their clients like ATMs, they decided it was time for a change!

NewEdj offers business advisory services to its clients but with a difference, they leave behind a tangible skills legacy so that the client receives not just the solution, but the know-how for the future.

Made in United States
Orlando, FL
11 November 2023